DK f ut!

TIMES TABLES

SUPPORTS THE NEW **NATIONAL** Curriculum

Consultant Sean McArdle

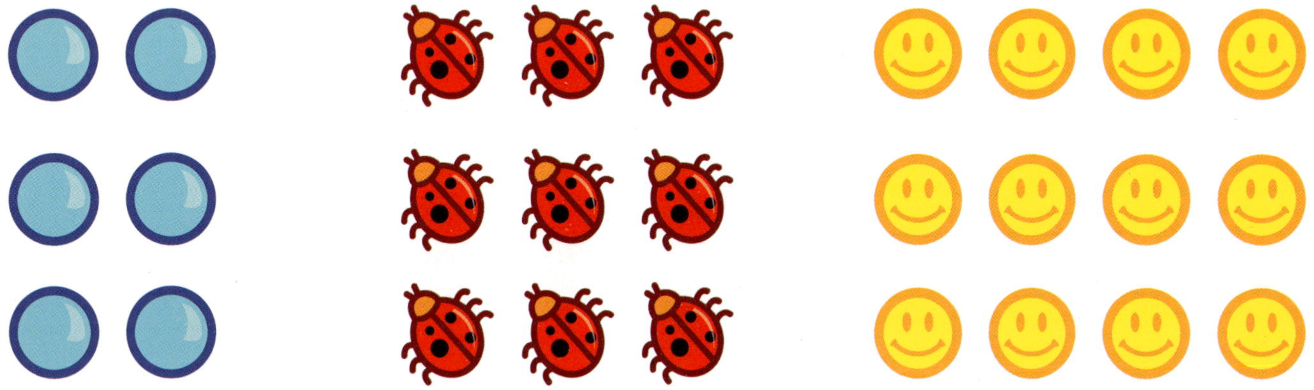

DK | Penguin Random House

Senior Editors Deborah Lock, Cécile Landau
Editor Nishtha Kapil
Asst. Editor Kritika Gupta
Art Editors Dheeraj Arora, Jyotsna Julka, Yamini Panwar, Kanika Kalra
DTP Designer Anita Yadav
Managing Editor Soma B. Chowdhury
Managing Art Editors Richard Czapnik, Ahlawat Gunjan
Art Director Martin Wilson
Producer, Pre-Production Gill Reid
Senior Producer Charlotte Oliver
Maths Consultant Sean McArdle
Design Consultant Shefali Upadhyay

This edition published in Great Britain in 2015 by
Dorling Kindersley Limited
80 Strand, London, WC2R 0RL

Material in this book was previously published in
10 Minutes A Day Times Tables (2014)

001—289211—06/15

A CIP catalogue record for this book
is available from the British Library
ISBN: 978-0-2412-4100-4

Printed and bound in Italy by L.E.G.O. S.p.A.

Contents

Extra challenge:
In these boxes are some extra challenges to extend your skills. You can do them after finishing the questions if you wish. Or, they can be stand-alone activities.

Groups of 2

Do not get the blues.
March in 2s.

1. Anne has 2 baskets with 5 flowers in each basket.
How many flowers are there in total?
Fill in the numbers.

☐ baskets x ☐ flowers = ☐ flowers

2. Complete each sequence:

2 4 6 ☐ ☐ ☐ 14 ☐ ☐ ☐ 22 ☐

48 46 44 ☐ ☐ ☐ ☐ ☐ ☐ ☐ ☐ 26

54 56 58 ☐ ☐ ☐ ☐ ☐ ☐ ☐ 74 ☐

3. Answer these questions:

Six multiplied by two is ☐

Seven times two is ☐

Nine groups of two are ☐

4. A theatre ticket costs £24.50.
How much will 2 tickets cost?

☐

5. Work out these multiplication sums:

150	175	236	348	427	519
x 2	x 2	x 2	x 2	x 2	x 2
....	....	....	....	....	....

Extra challenge:
Can you recite the 2x table backwards?
Time yourself to see how quick you can be.

6) Divide each number by 2:

76 ☐ 142 ☐ 178 ☐

7) Work out these division sums:

2)126 2)240 2)352 2)684 2)792

8) Fazir and Tira shared £7.80 equally between them.
How much money did each child receive?

☐

9) There were 284 bees in 2 hives. If there was an equal number in each hive, how many bees were there in 1 hive?

☐ bees

10) How many shapes are there in each group?

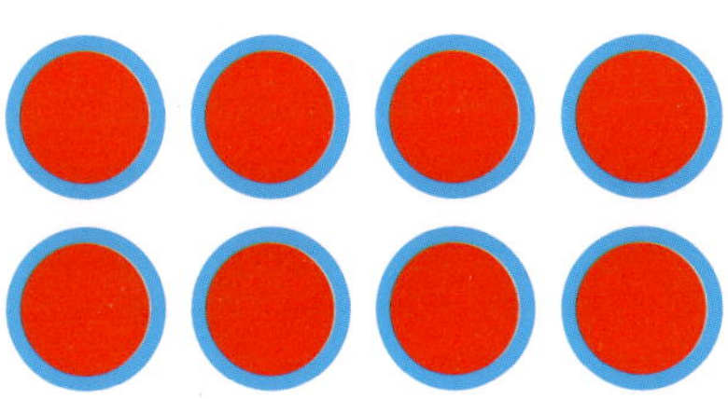

☐

☐

Pairs and doubles

Forget your troubles,
Forget your cares.
Practise doubles and pairs!

1. Double each number:

25 ☐ 42 ☐ 70 ☐ 127 ☐

2. How many socks are there in 36 pairs?

☐ socks

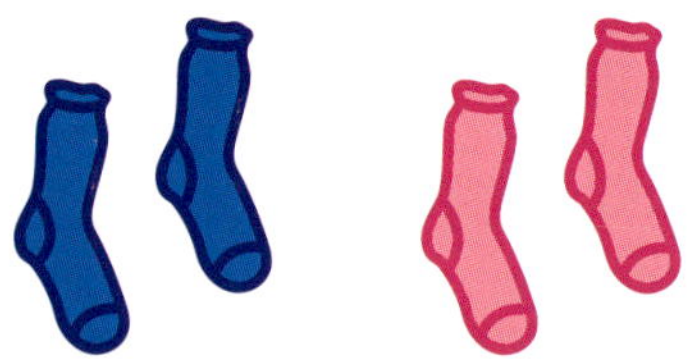

3. In a day, a factory makes wheels for 350 bicycles. How many wheels are made in 1 day?

☐ wheels

4. The table below shows some ingredients needed to make 12 biscuits. Calculate how much of each you will need to make 24 biscuits.
Hint: Double each amount.

Ingredients	Quantity for 12 biscuits	Quantity for 24 biscuits
Flour	350g (12oz)	
Eggs	2	
Butter	225g (8oz)	
Caster sugar	175g (6oz)	
Dark chocolate	350g (12oz)	
Light brown sugar	175g (6oz)	

Extra challenge:
I am thinking of a number between 1 and 10. I double it, double again and double yet again. My answer is 24. What number did I start with? Ask friends to do the same exercise with a different starting number. Can you work out what their starting number was?

5 How many wings do 275 crane flies have altogether?
Note: A crane fly has two wings.

[ ] wings

6 The chart shows the number of bunches of flowers sold in a store in one week. Write the total for each day.

✿ = 2 bunches

Day	Number of bunches sold	Total
Monday	10 x ✿	
Tuesday	8 x ✿	
Wednesday	12 x ✿	
Thursday	9 x ✿	
Friday	20 x ✿	
Saturday	14 x ✿	
Sunday	5 x ✿	

7 Ryan cycles 56km, but Jake cycles twice as far. How far does Jake cycle?

[ ]

8 Mum has spent £84.00 on presents for Jayden, but Dad has spent double that amount. How much money has Dad spent?

[ ]

Groups of 10

Count up in 10s
Again and again.

1. Tiya had 7 parcels. Each parcel weighed 10 kg. How much did the parcels weigh altogether?

2. Complete these sequences:

10	20	30							
150	140	130							
270	280	290							

3. Answer these questions:

Ten eights are

Ten times ten is

Nine multiplied by ten is

4. Zina saved 35 10-pence coins. How much money did Zina have altogether?

5. Work out these multiplication sums:

436	845	152	1 689	791	287
x 10	x 10	x 10	x 10	x 10	x 10

Extra challenge:
Think of a 2-digit number. Multiply the number by 10, multiply the same number by 20 and then the same number again by 30. Do you notice a pattern? To multiply your number by 40, try multiplying by 10 then multiplying the answer by 4.

6 Divide each number by 10:

10 ☐ 40 ☐ 80 ☐ 120 ☐ 150 ☐

7 Work out these division sums:

10)420 10)367 10)780 10)842 10)990

8 How many leaves are there in each group? **Hint:** Multiply the number of rows by the number of columns.

Multiplying by 100 and 1 000

Carefully count the zeros
To be a math superhero!

1 Multiply each number by 100:

4 ☐ 47 ☐ 470 ☐ 4 070 ☐

2 A box contains 100 T-shirts. How many T-shirts are there in 64 boxes?

☐ T-shirts

3 Multiply the number by 100 each time:

3 ☐ ☐ ☐

82 ☐ ☐ ☐

4 How many centimetres are there in 84 m? ☐

5 Divide each number by 100:

42 000 ☐ 702 000 ☐

804 200 ☐ 6 000 000 ☐

Extra challenge:

What is 30% of £1 500? Remember: 30% is the same as $\frac{30}{100}$.
So divide £1 500 by 100 and multiply by 30. It is sale time.
Calculate 20% of £80, 40% of £200, and 60% of £45.50.

6. Multiply each number by 1 000:

7 ☐ 82 ☐ 146 ☐ 150 ☐

7. How many grams are there in 7.2 kg?

☐

8. How many pence are there in £35?

☐

9. A plane flies at a height of 10 668 m.
What is this height in kilometres?

☐

10. A colony of army ants has 700 000 ants. As the ants cross a river, 20% of the colony dies. How many ants make it across?

☐ ants

Groups of 3

Count in groups of 3.
It is as easy as can be.

1 A jar holds 8 biscuits. How many biscuits are there in 3 jars?

[ ] biscuits

2 Complete each sequence:

0	3	6							
36	33	30							
36	39	42							

3 Answer these questions:

Three fives are [ ]

Three multiplied by seven is [ ]

Three times nine is [ ]

4 Neo bought 6 oranges at 30p each. What was the total cost of the 6 oranges?

[ ]

5 Work out these multiplication sums:

16	33	55	79	145	229
x 3	x 3	x 3	x 3	x 3	x 3
....	....	....	....	....	....

Extra challenge:
Say the 3x table to a rap beat. Singing the times tables helps to learn them. Try saying them to your own musical beats.

6 Divide each number by 3:

6 ☐ 15 ☐ 24 ☐ 36 ☐ 45 ☐

7 How long will it take Anita to save 42 p if she saves 3 p every week?

☐ weeks

8 Work out these division sums:

$3\overline{)60}$ $3\overline{)90}$ $3\overline{)72}$ $3\overline{)99}$ $3\overline{)183}$

9 Pablo was paid £3 for each car that he washed. He earned £39 in one week. How many cars did Pablo wash that week?

☐ cars

10 How many shapes are there in each group?

☐ ☐

Triple fun

Triple the fun!
Multiply x3 to get these done.

1. How many wealth are there on 15 tricycles?

   ______ wheels

2. How many sides do 55 triangles have?

   ______ sides

3. About 170 triplets are born in the United Kingdom each year. How many babies is this?

   ______ babies

4. Thirty-nine trimarans race in a competition. How many hulls are there altogether? **Note:** A trimaran is a boat with 3 hulls.

   ______ hulls

5. Fifty-four children are split into groups of 3. How many groups of children are there?

   ______ groups

6. A magnifying glass makes bugs look triple their size. Below are the original sizes of the bugs. What size is each of the bugs when it is magnified?

Worm: 6.5 cm ______

Centipede: 5.25 cm ______

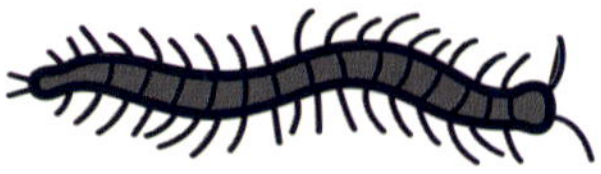

Ladybird: 1.75 cm ______

Extra challenge:
How many multiples of 3 are also the answer to other times tables? For example, 12 is a multiple of 3 and is also the answer to 1 x 12, 2 x 6 and 3 x 4. Make a list of all the overlaps.

7) Packets of biscuits are sold in boxes of 3 packets. This chart shows how many boxes are sold from a store in a week. Calculate the number of packets sold that week.  = 3 packets

Day	Number of boxes	Total
Monday		
Tuesday		
Wednesday		
Thursday	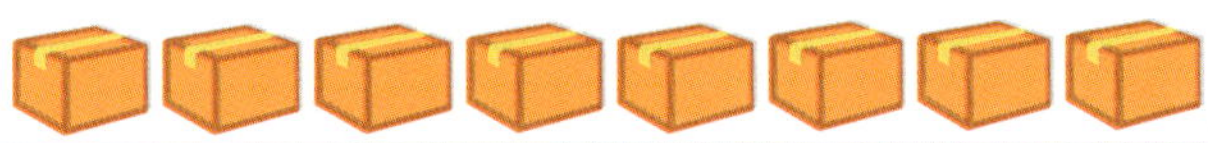	
Friday	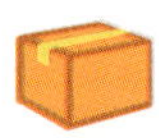	
Saturday	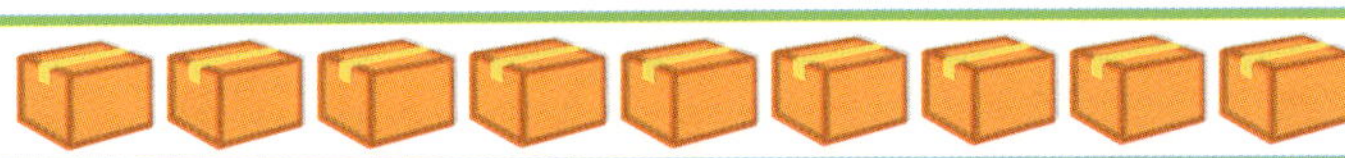	
Sunday	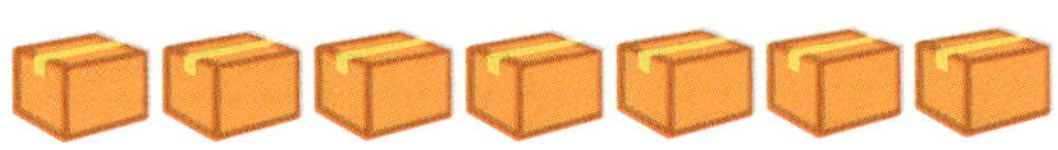	

8) Leaving no spaces, fit 9 small triangles (of equal size) inside the large equilateral triangle.

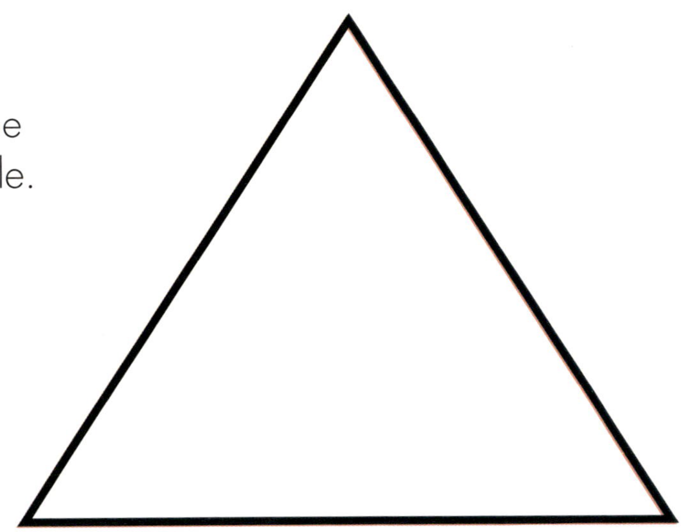

Groups of 4

Are you ready for more?
Here is counting in sets of 4.

1. Share 28 sweets equally among 4 children. How many sweets will each child get?

.... sweets

2. Complete each sequence:

0	4	8							
48	44	40							
52	56	60							

3. Answer these questions:

Nine times four is ....

Seven groups of four are ....

Four fives are ....

4. Dad took Devan, Jesse, and Owen to the fair. The roller coaster ride cost £1.50 for each person. How much did Dad have to pay for all of them to go on the ride?

....

5. Work out these multiplication sums:

23	17	25	115	200	214
x 4	x 4	x 4	x 4	x 4	x 4
....	....	....	....	....	....

Extra challenge:
Another way to work out the answer to 4 times a number is to multiply the number by 2 and then its answer by 2 again. Choose some numbers between 1 and 20 and give this a go.

6 Divide each number by 4:

0 ☐   4 ☐   16 ☐   36 ☐   48 ☐

7 Jeff buys a pack of 4 pencils. The pack costs £1.68. How much does 1 pencil cost?

☐

8 Work out these division sums:

$4\overline{)56}$ $4\overline{)96}$ $4\overline{)100}$ $4\overline{)128}$ $4\overline{)284}$

9 A box contains 24 chocolates. They are laid out in 4 equal rows. How many chocolates are there in each row?

☐ chocolates

10 How many shapes are there in each group?

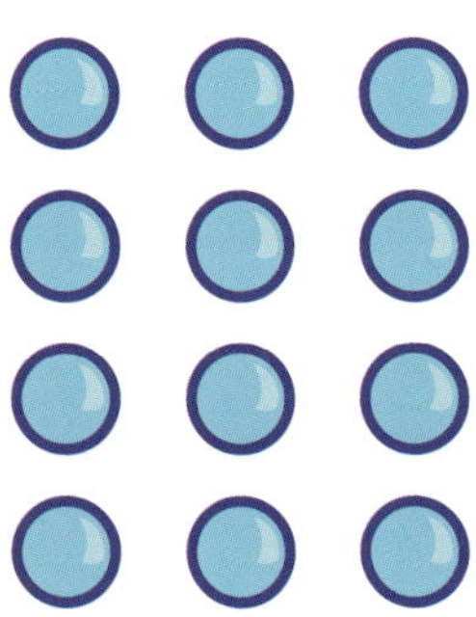

☐

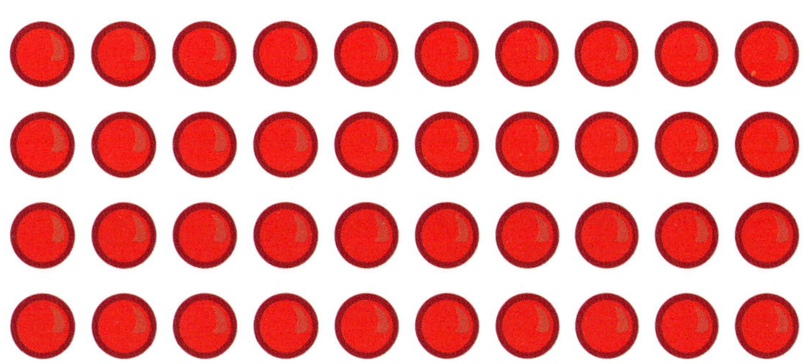

☐

Shapes

Count the angles and the sides,
Then read the question and multiply.

1 How many sides do these shapes have in total?

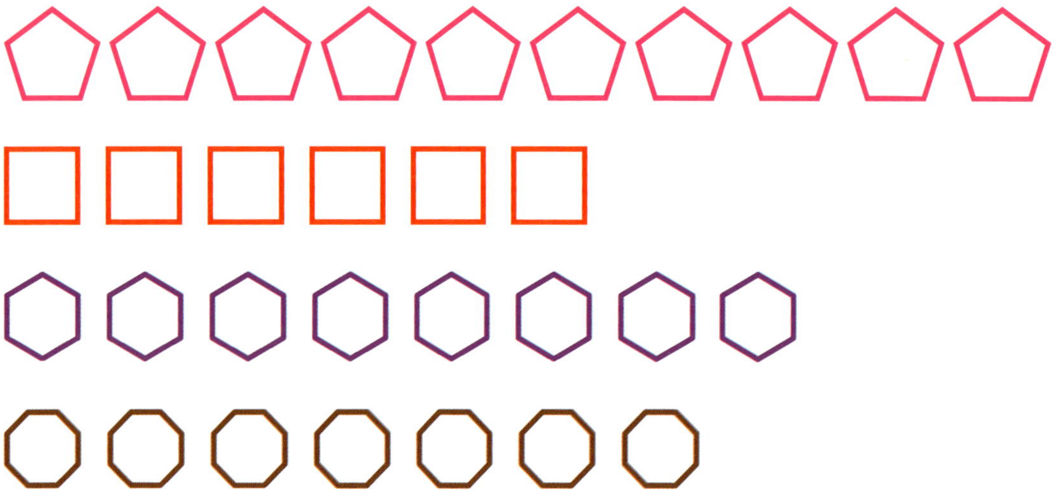

2 How many triangles have 27 angles in total?

triangles

3 The inside angles of an equilateral triangle add up to 180°. What is the value of each angle?

4 Each side of a regular hexagon is 7 cm. What is the perimeter of the hexagon?

5 What is the area of a rectangle with a length of 11 cm and a breadth of 4 cm?

6 Each angle of a square is 90°. What is the total of the 4 angles?

Extra challenge:
What times tables will help you solve these problems: What is the perimeter of a regular pentagon with 4-cm-long sides? What is the area of a square with 6-cm-long sides? What is the volume of a cube with 3-cm-long sides?

7 A cuboid has 8 vertices. How many cuboids will have a total of 80 vertices?

[ ] cuboids

8 How many faces do these shapes have?

7 triangular prisms [ ]

9 cuboids [ ]

12 cylinders [ ]

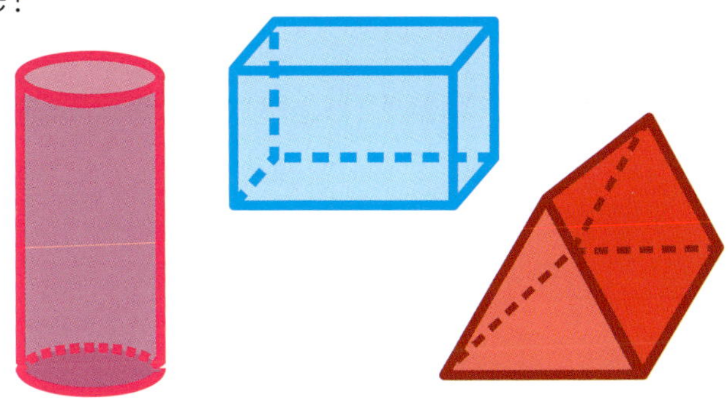

9 How many edges do these shapes have?

7 cubes [ ]

4 square-based pyramids [ ]

3 hexagonal prisms [ ]

10 What is the volume of this cuboid?
Hint: Volume = length x breadth x height

[ ]

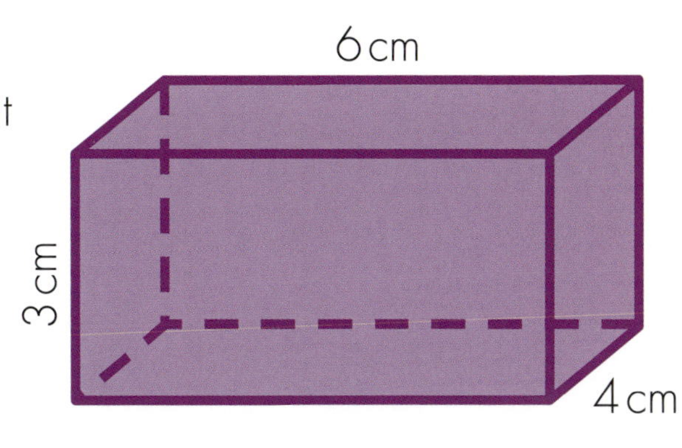

Groups of 5

Are you ready to dive
Into counting in 5s?

1. A pack of greeting cards contains 5 cards. How many cards are there in 3 packs?

   ☐ cards

2. Complete each sequence:

0	5	10	☐	☐	☐	☐	☐	☐	☐
60	55	50	☐	☐	☐	☐	☐	☐	☐
75	80	85	☐	☐	☐	☐	☐	☐	☐

3. Answer these questions:

   Five groups of six are ☐

   Seven multiplied by five is ☐

   Eleven times five is ☐

4. David saved 24 5-pence coins. How much money did David save?

   ☐

5. Work out these multiplication sums:

18	20	49	56	130	222
x 5	x 5	x 5	x 5	x 5	x 5
....	....	....	....	....	....

Extra challenge:
Calculate the total of the following amounts:

- 5 x 10p
- 5 x 5p
- 20 x 5p
- 25p ÷ 5
- 5 x 25p
- 15 x 5p
- 50 x 5p
- £1 ÷ 5

6. Divide each number by 5:

10 ☐ 25 ☐ 30 ☐ 50 ☐ 85 ☐

7. Five children are given £1.95 to share equally among them. How much money will each child receive? ☐

8. Work out these division sums:

5) 65 5) 80 5) 125 5) 175 5) 250

9. There are 270 children in a school. There are 5 years, and each year has an equal number of children. How many children are there in Year 4? ☐ children

10. How many shapes are there in each group?

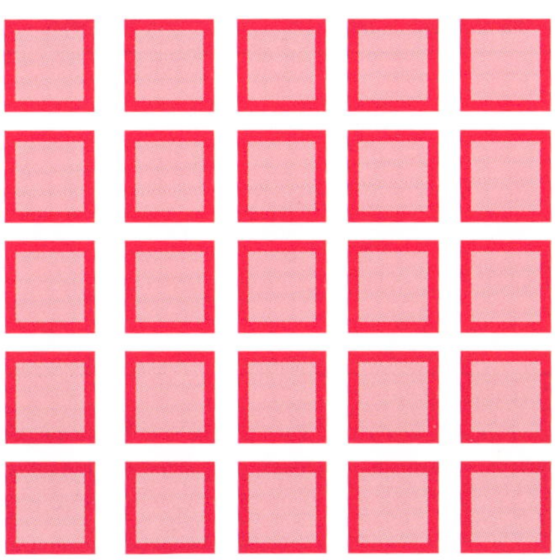

Telling the time

Tick tock! Tick tock!
Ready to go? Then start the clock.

1) How many minutes are there in 4 hours?

2) How many minutes is it past 11 o'clock?

3) How many minutes are there between 9.45 a.m. and 11.05 a.m.?

4) How many minutes are there in 1 day?

5) How many decades are there in half a century?
Note: A decade is 10 years; a century is 100 years.

decades

Extra challenge:
If a watch is 5 minutes fast, what is the actual time if it reads: 9:55? 6:40? 2:20? 3:00? If a watch is 5 minutes slow, what is the actual time if it reads: 4:25? 7:00? 11:15? 12:00?

6 How many hours are there in these months?

September (30 days) ______ February (28 days) ______

May (31 days) ______

7 Write the number of minutes past the hour shown on each of these clocks.

______ ______ ______ ______

8 How many minutes are there between 3.10 p.m. and 5.25 p.m.?

______

Beat the clock 1

This is the place to gather pace.
How many answers do you know?
Get ready, get set and go!

1 0 x 3 =	2 12 x 2 =	3 9 x 5 =
4 1 x 4 =	5 11 x 5 =	6 3 x 4 =
7 7 x 3 =	8 10 x 2 =	9 2 x 2 =
10 6 x 5 =	11 11 x 4 =	12 8 x 2 =
13 4 x 4 =	14 10 x 5 =	15 2 x 5 =
16 6 x 3 =	17 10 x 9 =	18 9 x 4 =
19 1 x 5 =	20 12 x 4 =	21 6 x 4 =
22 7 x 4 =	23 10 x 1 =	24 12 x 10 =
25 2 x 4 =	26 10 x 7 =	27 10 x 10 =
28 8 x 4 =	29 11 x 2 =	30 0 x 2 =

Time challenge:
Set the clock ticking and see how fast and accurately you can work out the answers! Remember, you can return to this page again and again to improve your score.

(31) 24 ÷ 3 = ☐	(32) 6 ÷ 2 = ☐	(33) 15 ÷ 5 = ☐
(34) 30 ÷ 5 = ☐	(35) 9 ÷ 3 = ☐	(36) 30 ÷ 10 = ☐
(37) 14 ÷ 2 = ☐	(38) 3 ÷ 3 = ☐	(39) 50 ÷ 10 = ☐
(40) 40 ÷ 5 = ☐	(41) 2 ÷ 2 = ☐	(42) 90 ÷ 10 = ☐
(43) 21 ÷ 3 = ☐	(44) 6 ÷ 3 = ☐	(45) 10 ÷ 10 = ☐
(46) 18 ÷ 2 = ☐	(47) 27 ÷ 3 = ☐	(48) 80 ÷ 10 = ☐
(49) 15 ÷ 5 = ☐	(50) 15 ÷ 3 = ☐	(51) 60 ÷ 10 = ☐
(52) 40 ÷ 8 = ☐	(53) 36 ÷ 3 = ☐	(54) 70 ÷ 10 = ☐
(55) 18 ÷ 3 = ☐	(56) 60 ÷ 5 = ☐	(57) 110 ÷ 10 = ☐
(58) 30 ÷ 3 = ☐	(59) 25 ÷ 5 = ☐	(60) 100 ÷ 10 = ☐

Groups of 6

6, 12, 18, 24:
Count in 6s to make numbers more.

1. A tube holds 6 tennis balls. How many balls will 8 tubes hold?

☐ balls

2. Complete each sequence:

0	6	12	☐	☐	☐	☐	☐	☐	☐
72	66	60	☐	☐	☐	☐	☐	☐	☐
54	60	66	☐	☐	☐	☐	☐	☐	☐

3. Answer these questions:

Six threes are ☐

Four multiplied by six is ☐

Six groups of seven are ☐

4. Selma bought 9 bananas at 6p each. How much money did she spend?

☐

5. Work out these multiplication sums:

14	25	38	54	116	200
x 6	x 6	x 6	x 6	x 6	x 6
....	....	....	....	....	....

Extra challenge:

Another way to work out the answer to 6x a number is to multiply the number by 3 and then double the answer. Choose some numbers between 1 and 20 and give this a go.

6 Divide each number by 6:

18 ☐   30 ☐   66 ☐   72 ☐   96 ☐

7 £2.50 is shared equally among 6 children. How much money is left over?

☐

8 174 cars are parked in 6 rows of equal length. How many cars are there in each row?

☐ cars

9 Work out these division sums:

$6\overline{)90}$ $6\overline{)102}$ $6\overline{)204}$ $6\overline{)276}$ $6\overline{)348}$

10 How many items are there in each group?

☐ cabbages

☐ strawberries

Bugs

Multiply creepy-crawlies' legs
And then count up the butterfly eggs.

1) Will recorded the number of bugs he saw in his garden in a month. How many legs did each type of insect have altogether?
Hint: An insect has 6 legs.

Name of bug	Number sighted	Total number of legs
Beetle	~~||||~~ ~~||||~~ ~~||||~~ ||	
Wasp	~~||||~~ |||	
Butterfly	~~||||~~ ~~||||~~ ~~||||~~	
Ladybird	~~||||~~ ~~||||~~ ~~||||~~ ~~||||~~ |	

2) If a desert locust eats 2 g of food each day, how much will a swarm of 66 million desert locusts eat in a day?

3) A ladybird is about 6 mm long. Under the microscope, the ladybird is magnified 40 times. What size is the ladybird when seen through the microscope?

4) A leaf-cutter ant travels 360 m each day. Altogether, what is the total distance the ant will travel in 60 days?

Extra challenge:
A queen honey bee lays 1 500 eggs per day. How many eggs does she lay in 1 month (30 days)? How many eggs does she lay in 6 months (180 days)?

5 How many wings does a swarm of 6 000 bees have altogether?
Hint: Bees have 4 wings.

[ ] wings

6 A queen wasp can lay 2 000 eggs a day. How many eggs can she lay in 60 days?

[ ] eggs

7 A butterfly lays 600 eggs, and only a quarter of them hatch into caterpillars. How many eggs **do not** hatch?

[ ] eggs

8 Class 5F went to a pond. They made a picture chart of the number of bugs they saw in the pond. How many bugs of each type did they see?

 = 6 bugs  = 3 bugs

Name of bug	Number of bugs	Total
Pond skaters	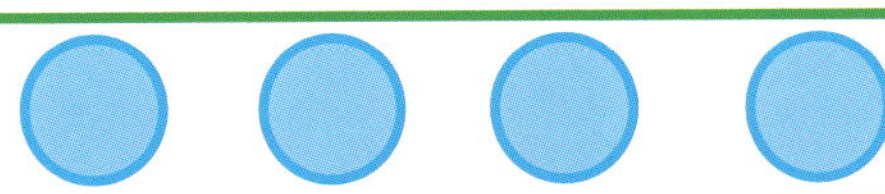	
Water bugs		
Whirligig beetles	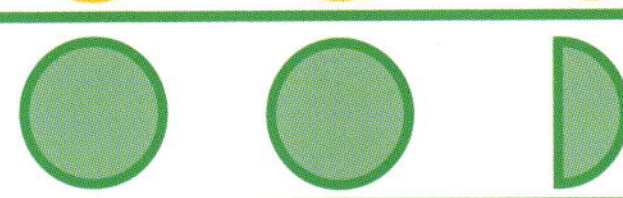	
Dragonfly nymphs		
Water spiders		

Sports

Jump, throw, kick, and dash.
You will have this page done in a flash!

1) Adam ran 400 m in 59 seconds. Jonas took twice as long. How long did Jonas take?

2) Three cyclists raced at 58 mph, 63 mph, and 56 mph. What was their average speed?

3) These were the results of a season's football games:
A win = 5 points, a draw = 3 points, and a loss = 1 point.
How many points did each team get?

Football team	Win	Loss	Draw	Points
England	8	2	5	
United States	7	3	6	
Japan	7	1	7	
Brazil	9	2	4	

4) The winner of a tennis tournament won 4 times the prize money of a semi-finalist. If a semi-finalist received £475 000, how much money did the winner receive?

Extra challenge:
Seven competitors ran a 100 m race in a total time of 91 seconds. What was their average time?

5 John threw a javelin a distance of 64 m. Amy threw the javelin an eighth ($\frac{1}{8}$) less than John's distance. How far did Amy throw?

6 Seven race car drivers have a total of 1 645 points. What is the average number of points scored?

points

7 There were 162 rounders players taking part in a tournament. Each team had 9 players. How many teams were there?

teams

8 The length of a swimming pool is 25 m. This chart shows how many times each child swam that length. How far did each child swim?

Name of child	Number of lengths	Total distance
Harry	10	
Jasmine	8	
Jamie	6	
Heidi	5	

Groups of 7

7, 14, 21, 28:
Get started, do not wait!

1) A dog eats 3 dog treats a day.
How many treats will it eat in 7 days?

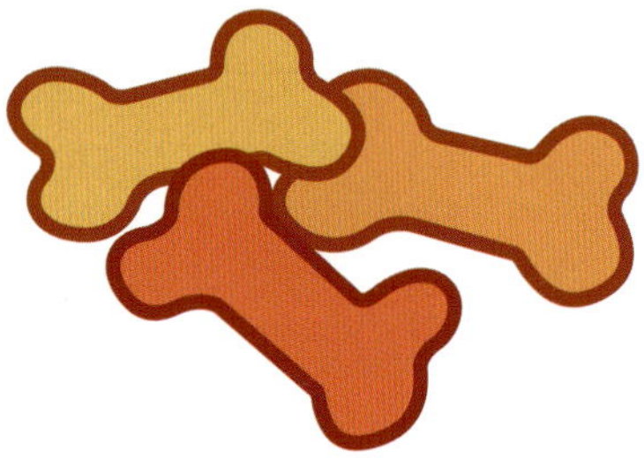

[ ] treats

2) Complete each sequence:

0	7	14							
84	77	70							
35	42	49							

3) Answer these questions:

Seven sixes are [ ]

Eight multiplied by seven is [ ]

Five groups of seven are [ ]

4) A train ticket costs £7.
How much will 6 tickets cost?

[ ]

5) Work out these multiplication sums:

14	20	35	59	123	246
x 7	x 7	x 7	x 7	x 7	x 7
....	....	....	....	....	....

Extra challenge:
Another way to work out or check the answer to 7x a number is to multiply the number by 5, multiply the same number by 2 and then add the two answers. For example: 9 x 7 = (9 x 5) + (9 x 2) = 45 + 18 = 63. Choose a number between 1 and 20 and give this a go.

6) Divide each number by 7:

0 ☐   21 ☐   49 ☐   77 ☐   98 ☐

7) Seven books cost £35.84 altogether. If each book was the same price, what was the price of 1 book? ☐

8) Work out these division sums:

$7\overline{)84}$ $7\overline{)140}$ $7\overline{)105}$ $7\overline{)133}$ $7\overline{)224}$

9) Share 42 chairs equally around 7 tables. How many chairs will you keep around each table? ☐ chairs

10) How many shapes are there in each group?

☐

☐

Days of the week

Days 7; months 12; weeks 52;
Times tables are fun all year through.

1 How many days are there in 15 weeks?

[ ] days

2 How many weeks are there in 7 years?

[ ] weeks

3 How many hours are there in a week?

[ ]

4 Dad works 35 hours a week. How many hours does he work over 4 weeks?

[ ]

5 Fran cycles for 30 minutes every day. How many minutes does she cycle in one week?

[ ]

6 A bookshop opens for 7 hours each day from Monday to Saturday. How many hours is it open in one week?

[ ]

Extra challenge:
A swimming team exercised 1 hour a day, swam 3 hours a day, and ran 2 hours a day. How many hours did they exercise, swim, and run in 1 week, in 4 weeks, and in 1 year?

7 Chris practises on the keyboard for 105 minutes every week.
He does an equal amount of time every day.
How long is each practice?

8 Ella travelled for 91 days. How many weeks is this?

weeks

9 Dad books a holiday 22 weeks before going.
How many days does the family have to wait?

days

10 How long in minutes does Kim do these daily activities in one week?

Watching 45 minutes of television

Playing 30 minutes of computer games

Reading for 1 hour 10 minutes

Dice and cards

Playing with dice and cards is fun
When your multiplication work is done.

1 Multiply the two numbers shown on the dice:

2 Add the numbers shown on the dice, and then multiply your answer by 6.

3 Jack threw a double six 5 times.
What was his total?

4 These are the scores of four players. They each need to throw a double to reach 100 points. What is the number that needs to appear on both dice for each player? Fill in the spaces in the table.

Player	Score	Number required on both dice
1	90	
2	98	
3	94	
4	88	

Extra challenge:
Calculate these answers:
- the product of 7 diamonds, 5 diamonds, and 4 diamonds;
- the product of 8 spades, 6 spades, and 2 spades;
- the product of 5 hearts, 9 hearts, and 3 hearts.

5) Jess throws a die 100 times and records her scores. What is the total amount scored altogether by Jess? Fill in the spaces in the table.

Number on die	Number of times thrown	Total
1	𝍸 𝍸 𝍸 |	
2	𝍸 𝍸 𝍸 𝍸	
3	𝍸 𝍸 𝍸 |||	
4	𝍸 𝍸 𝍸	
5	𝍸 𝍸 𝍸 ||	
6	𝍸 𝍸 ||||	
	Total	

6) A full deck of cards has 13 cards of each suit.

Note: There are 4 suits in a deck.

How many cards are there in a deck? ☐ cards

How many cards are there in

4 decks? ☐ cards

9 decks? ☐ cards

6 decks? ☐ cards

Multiply each of these cards by 8:

9 hearts ☐

8 diamonds ☐

Queen (12) clubs ☐

Groups of 8

**Get started now and do not be late!
Make steady progress as you count in 8s.**

1. Six trains run every hour. Each train pulls 8 carriages. How many carriages are pulled every hour?

   ☐ carriages

2. Complete these sequences:

0	8	16	☐	☐	☐	☐	☐	☐	☐
96	88	80	☐	☐	☐	☐	☐	☐	☐
40	48	56	☐	☐	☐	☐	☐	☐	☐

3. Answer these questions:

   Eight sixes are ☐

   Two multiplied by eight is ☐

   Nine times eight is ☐

4. A bag of apples costs £1.46. How much will 8 bags cost?

   ☐

5. Work out these multiplication sums:

15	24	48	97	120	236
x 8	x 8	x 8	x 8	x 8	x 8
....	....	....	....	....	....

Extra challenge:
Another way to work out the answer to 8x a number is to multiply the number by 4 and then double the answer; or double the number, double the answer, and double again. Choose some numbers between 1 and 20 and give both these ways a go.

6) Work out these division sums:

8) 96   8) 144   8) 168   8) 256   8) 312

7) Tammy needs 192 m of fencing to go around her garden. Each fencing panel is 8 m long. How many panels will she need?

panels

8) Perry pays £2.80 for 8 pencils. How much did 1 pencil cost?

9) Divide each number by 8:

0   24   56   80   96

10) How many gems are there in each group?

Solar system

5, 4, 3, 2, 1;
Blast off into space to get these done.

1. Thirty-five satellites are launched into orbit each year. How many satellites have been launched in 8 years?

[ ] satellites

2. A probe travelling at 500 mph will take 8 years to get to Mars. How fast does the probe need to travel to get there in 1 year?

[ ]

3. Mars takes approximately 687 days to orbit the Sun. How many days will it take for Mars to orbit the Sun 8 times?

[ ] days

4. Neptune takes 165 years to orbit the Sun. How many years will it take to go around the Sun 8 times?

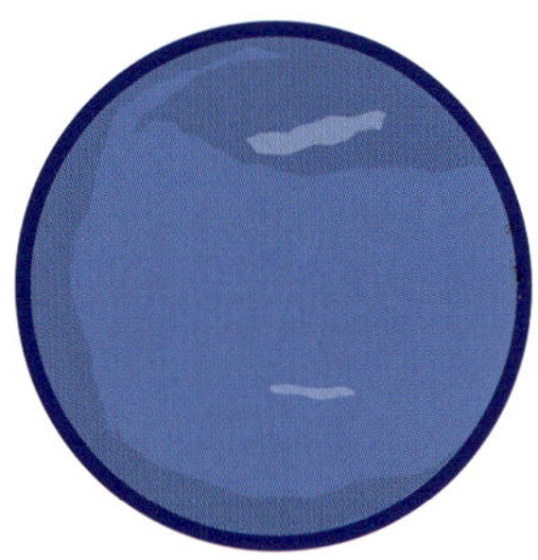

[ ] years

5. Mercury takes 88 Earth days to orbit the Sun. How many times will Mercury go around the Sun in 880 Earth days?

[ ] times

Extra challenge:
A team of 7 astronauts prepare for an 8-day space mission. If they each need 1.7 kg of food per day and 2 litres of water, what is the minimum amount they need to take with them?

6 Multiply the 8 moons of Neptune with the 16 moons of Jupiter.

[ ] moons

7 The midday surface temperature of Mercury is 420°C. What is 8 times hotter than the surface of Mercury?

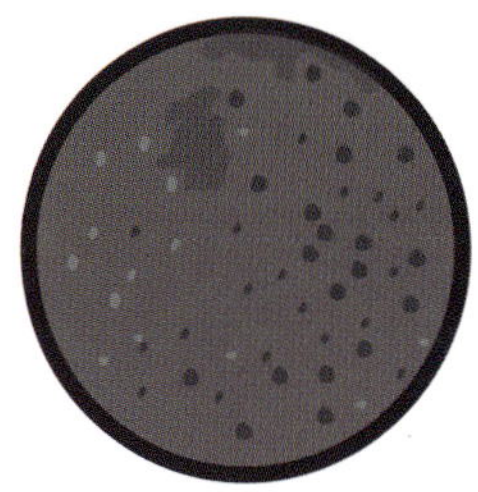

[ ]

8 Mercury is 4 878 km in diameter. What is an eighth ($\frac{1}{8}$) of its diameter?

[ ]

9 One day on Saturn lasts 10 hours and 14 minutes on Earth. How long in Earth time will 8 days on Saturn last?

[ ]

One day on Uranus lasts 17 hours and 8 minutes on Earth. How long in Earth time will 8 days on Saturn last?

[ ]

10 Saturn is 1.4 billion km away from the Sun. What is $\frac{5}{8}$ of this distance?

[ ]

Jupiter is 780 million km away from the Sun. What is $\frac{3}{8}$ of this distance?

[ ]

Fractions

**Split the whole by the denominator,
Then multiply by the numerator.**

1) What is half ($\frac{1}{2}$) of each number?

18 ☐ 10 ☐ 6 ☐ 24 ☐

2) What is a third ($\frac{1}{3}$) of each amount?

12g ☐ 27g ☐ 33g ☐ 42g ☐

3) What is a quarter ($\frac{1}{4}$) of each number?

4 ☐ 20 ☐ 36 ☐ 52 ☐

4) There are 60 carrots in a box.
How many carrots make up...

$\frac{7}{10}$ of the box? ☐ carrots

$\frac{1}{10}$ of the box? ☐ carrots

$\frac{2}{10}$ of the box? ☐ carrots

5) There were 25 bananas, and $\frac{1}{5}$ were eaten.
How many bananas are left?

☐ bananas

Extra challenge:
Calculate the following amounts: $\frac{5}{9}$ of 450 g; $\frac{7}{10}$ of £2.50; $\frac{3}{8}$ of 640 cm. Write some fraction challenges for your friends. Did they get them right?

6 What is three quarters ($\frac{3}{4}$) of each number?

12 ☐ 24 ☐ 32 ☐ 44 ☐

7 What is $\frac{1}{8}$ of 48 slices of pizza?

☐ slices

8 What is $\frac{7}{10}$ of 40?

☐

9 There are 30 children in a class. $\frac{3}{5}$ of the class have school dinners. How many children **do not** have school dinners?

☐ children

10 Oliver picked 54 apples. $\frac{1}{6}$ were rotten. How many apples were rotten?

☐ apples

Groups of 9

**Wide awake and ready to shine?
Here is counting in sets of nine.**

1 There are 8 horse races in a day. If 9 different horses took part in each race, how many horses ran that day?

[ ] horses

2 Complete each sequence:

0	9	18							
108	99	90							
45	54	63							

3 Answer these questions:

Three multiplied by nine is [ ]

Nine eights are [ ]

Six groups of nine are [ ]

4 A bunch of flowers costs £4.99. How much will 9 bunches cost?

[ ]

5 Work out these multiplication sums:

16	23	92	47	150	218
x 9	x 9	x 9	x 9	x 9	x 9
....	....	....	....	....	....

Extra challenge:
Another way to work out the answer to 9x a number is to multiply the number by 10 and then take away the number from the answer. For example, 15 x 9 = (15 x 10) – 15 = 135. Choose some 2-digit numbers and give this a go.

6. Divide each number by 9:

9 ☐ 36 ☐ 45 ☐ 90 ☐ 108 ☐

7. Jake needed £468 to buy a new television. He decided to save an equal amount over 9 weeks to reach the total. What is the amount he needed to save each week?

☐

8. How many shapes are there in each group?

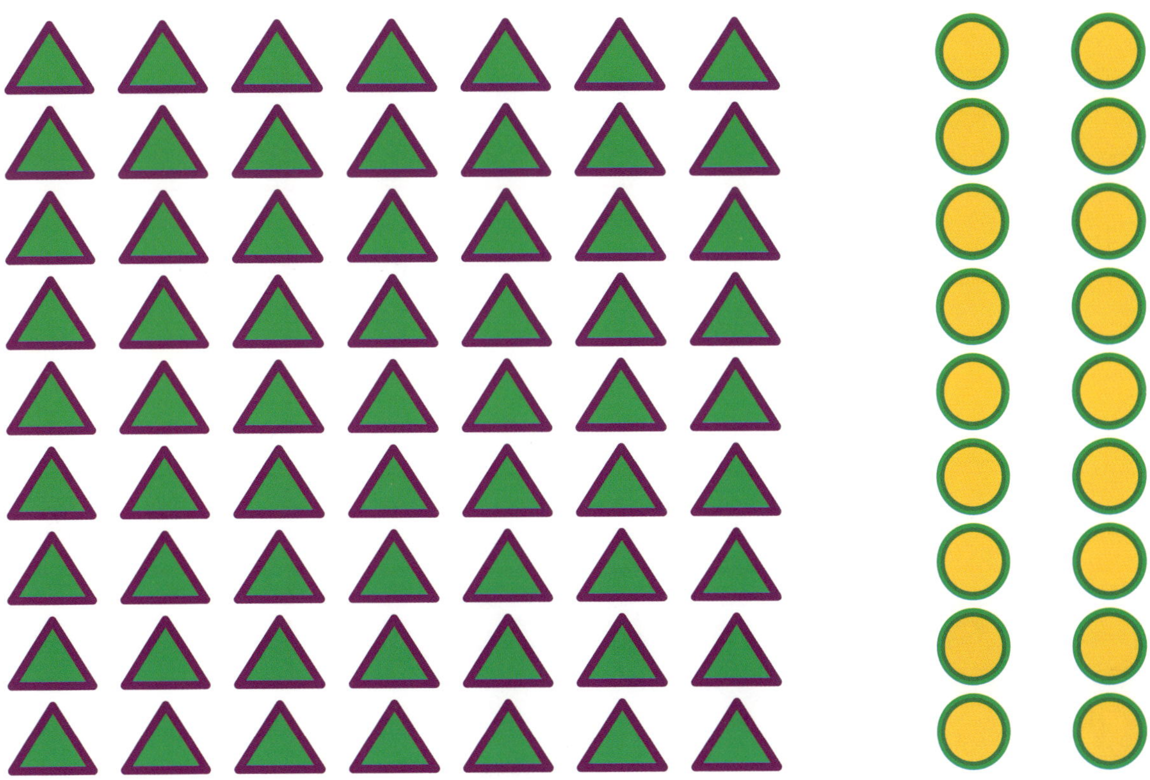

☐ ☐

Shopping

Pick, choose and weigh;
Then go to the checkout to pay!

1 Calculate the total cost that Karl spent shopping.

Item	Cost per item	Amount	Total
Tomatoes	20p	6	
Carrots	10p	8	
Cabbage	89p	2	
Peppers	43p	5	
Cheese	£1.26	1	
Bread	76p	3	
Juice	£1.49	4	
Milk	72p	6	
Biscuits	89p	7	
Pasta	£2.56	2	

Extra challenge:
Calculate the total of these amounts: 3 kg of apples at 45p a kilogram; 7 oranges at 23p each; 6 cans of soup at £1.20 a can. Which is cheaper? 12 packets of biscuits at 54p each or 9 jars of jam at 63p each?

2. A shopkeeper sold 6 red coats at £89 each. How much did the red coats cost altogether?

3. Mum bought 3 bracelets at £7.84 each. How much money did Mum spend?

4. Tami spent £77.97 on 3 pairs of shoes. Each pair cost the same amount. How much did each pair cost?

5. In a sale, the cost of a hat was reduced by 20%. The original price of the hat was £14.50. How much was it reduced by?

Division

Use your times tables know-how
To work out division questions now.

1 Match each question to its answer:

168 ÷ 6	524 ÷ 4	595 ÷ 7	729 ÷ 9
85	81	28	131

2 Use the long division method to work out each sum:

4 ⟌ 648   2 ⟌ 496   5 ⟌ 760   6 ⟌ 822

3 What is the remainder each time?

592 ÷ 3 ☐   264 ÷ 7 ☐

786 ÷ 4 ☐   543 ÷ 9 ☐

4 Circle all the multiples of 7:

14   23   35   43   76   84

Extra challenge:
How many multiples of 9 are also the answer to other times tables? For example, 18 is a multiple of 9 and is also the answer to 1 x 18, 2 x 9 and 3 x 6. Make a list of all the overlaps.

5 Circle all the multiples of 9:

28 54 61 83 99 108

6 Circle all the multiples of 12:

24 45 60 56 72 98 132

7 Work out these money sums:

£14.58 ÷ 3 =

£35.60 ÷ 8 =

£26.96 ÷ 4 =

£66.69 ÷ 9 =

8 List all the factors for each number:

24

36

72

100

Beat the clock 2

This is the place to gather pace.
How many answers do you know?
Get ready, get set, and go!

1) 0 x 9 = ☐ 2) 0 x 6 = ☐ 3) 8 x 9 = ☐

4) 5 x 8 = ☐ 5) 7 x 8 = ☐ 6) 3 x 8 = ☐

7) 2 x 9 = ☐ 8) 7 x 6 = ☐ 9) 2 x 7 = ☐

10) 1 x 7 = ☐ 11) 9 x 9 = ☐ 12) 10 x 9 = ☐

13) 2 x 8 = ☐ 14) 1 x 8 = ☐ 15) 12 x 6 = ☐

16) 3 x 6 = ☐ 17) 9 x 7 = ☐ 18) 10 x 7 = ☐

19) 4 x 7 = ☐ 20) 4 x 9 = ☐ 21) 11 x 6 = ☐

22) 8 x 8 = ☐ 23) 6 x 8 = ☐ 24) 11 x 8 = ☐

25) 9 x 6 = ☐ 26) 6 x 7 = ☐ 27) 12 x 7 = ☐

28) 5 x 6 = ☐ 29) 7 x 7 = ☐ 30) 12 x 9 = ☐

Time challenge:
Set the clock ticking and see how fast and accurately you can work out the answers! Remember, you can return to this page again and again to improve your score.

(31) $0 \div 7 =$ ☐ (32) $60 \div 6 =$ ☐ (33) $63 \div 9 =$ ☐

(34) $0 \div 8 =$ ☐ (35) $99 \div 9 =$ ☐ (36) $84 \div 7 =$ ☐

(37) $9 \div 9 =$ ☐ (38) $27 \div 9 =$ ☐ (39) $48 \div 8 =$ ☐

(40) $6 \div 6 =$ ☐ (41) $96 \div 8 =$ ☐ (42) $72 \div 8 =$ ☐

(43) $21 \div 7 =$ ☐ (44) $32 \div 8 =$ ☐ (45) $63 \div 7 =$ ☐

(46) $24 \div 6 =$ ☐ (47) $45 \div 9 =$ ☐ (48) $35 \div 7 =$ ☐

(49) $77 \div 7 =$ ☐ (50) $48 \div 6 =$ ☐ (51) $54 \div 9 =$ ☐

(52) $80 \div 8 =$ ☐ (53) $49 \div 7 =$ ☐ (54) $12 \div 6 =$ ☐

(55) $36 \div 6 =$ ☐ (56) $64 \div 8 =$ ☐ (57) $56 \div 7 =$ ☐

(58) $40 \div 8 =$ ☐ (59) $81 \div 9 =$ ☐ (60) $108 \div 9 =$ ☐

Groups of 11

11, 22, 33, 44;
Follow the pattern to find more.

1. A farmer plants 6 rows of tulips, with 11 bulbs in each row. How many tulip bulbs are planted?

   .... bulbs

2. Complete each sequence:

0	11	22							
143	132	121							
66	77	88							

3. Answer these questions:

   Eleven fours are ....

   Eleven groups of seven are ....

   Twelve times eleven is ....

4. Ellie buys 11 T-shirts at £1.10 each. How much does Ellie pay for 11 T-shirts?

   ....

5. Work out these multiplication sums:

14	25	69	33	81	100
x 11	x 11	x 11	x 11	x 11	x 11
......	......	......	......	......	......

Extra challenge:
Another way to work out or check the answer to 11x a number is to multiply the number by 10 and then add on the number to the answer. For example, 23 x 11 = (23 x 10) + 23 = 253. Choose some 2-digit numbers and give this a go.

6 Divide each number by 11:

22 ☐ 88 ☐ 121 ☐ 143 ☐ 176 ☐

7 Work out these division sums:

$11\overline{)187}$ ☐ $11\overline{)297}$ ☐ $11\overline{)363}$ ☐ $11\overline{)572}$ ☐ $11\overline{)781}$ ☐

8 How many spots are there in each group?

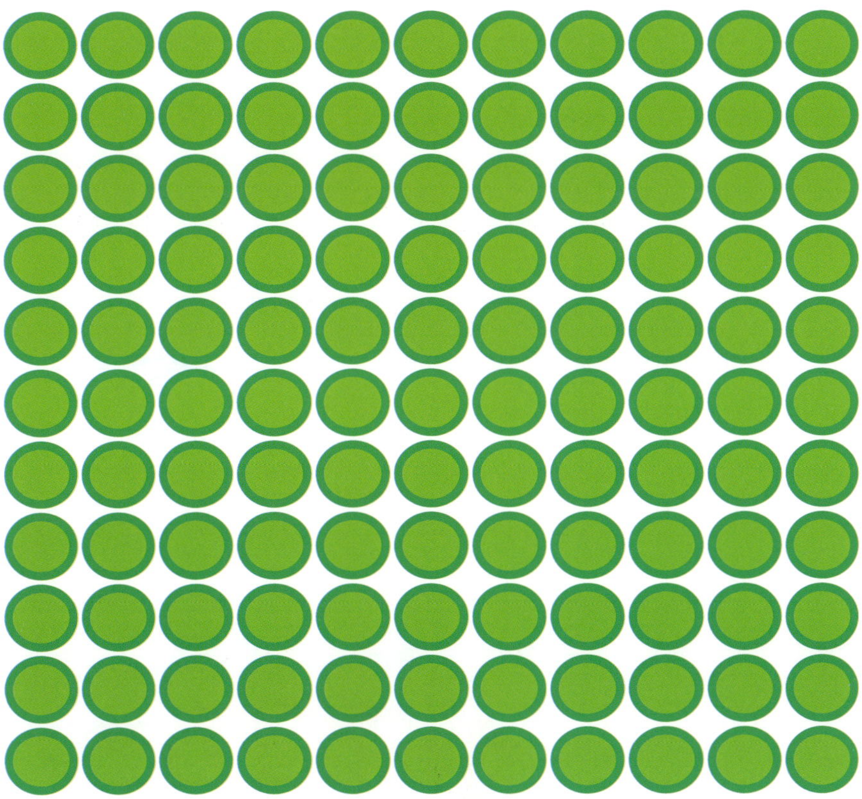
☐

☐

Buildings

**Count the windows, stairs and doors;
Multiply them by the number of floors.**

1. Each stairway of an apartment building has 12 steps. How many steps are there in 6 stairways?

   [ ] steps

2. A window cleaner takes 1 hour to clean 20 windows. How long will it take him to clean 120 windows?

   [ ]

3. There are 210 windows in a 7-storey office building. There is an equal number of windows on each storey. How many windows are there on the fifth storey?

   [ ] windows

4. An apartment building has 15 storeys and 6 flats on each storey. How many flats are there altogether?

   [ ] flats

5. A school has 4 blocks with 9 classrooms in each block. How many classrooms are there altogether?

   [ ] classrooms

Extra challenge:
If a 72-storey skyscraper has 100 windows, 63 offices, and 7 meeting rooms on each storey, how many windows, offices, and meeting rooms are there in total?

6) A builder uses 500 tiles to cover half a roof of a house. How many tiles will he need for 6 houses?

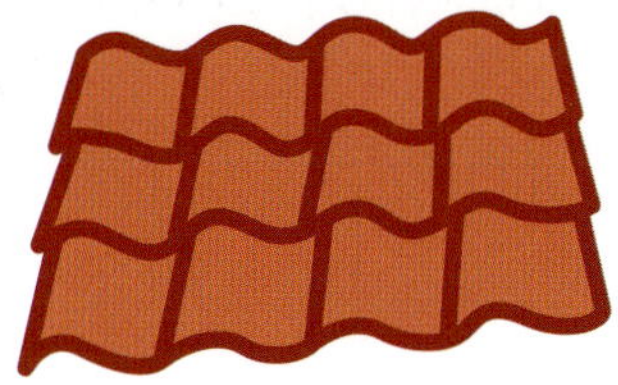

[ ] tiles

7) A 10-storey hotel has a total of 378 rooms. The rooms are on floors 2 to 10. If there is an equal number of rooms on each floor, how many rooms are there on the eighth floor?

[ ] rooms

8) A house costs £285 000. The estate agent receives 5% of the sale price. How much money does the agent receive?

[ ]

9) Two-thirds ($\frac{2}{3}$) of the 126 houses on Grove Avenue have garages. How many houses **do not** have garages?

[ ] houses

10) A shop has an area of 620 m^2. If the width of the shop is 20 m, what is its length?

[ ]

Sequences

Find the number pattern for each row;
The times tables facts are fun to know.

1 Fill in the missing numbers in each sequence:

5 10 ☐ ☐ ☐ 30 ☐ ☐ 45 ☐

60 ☐ ☐ 75 ☐ ☐ ☐ 95 ☐ 105

2 Complete each sequence:

4 8 12 ☐ ☐ ☐ ☐ ☐ ☐ ☐

7 14 21 ☐ ☐ ☐ ☐ ☐ ☐ ☐

25 50 75 ☐ ☐ ☐ ☐ ☐ ☐ ☐

3 Continue this pattern:

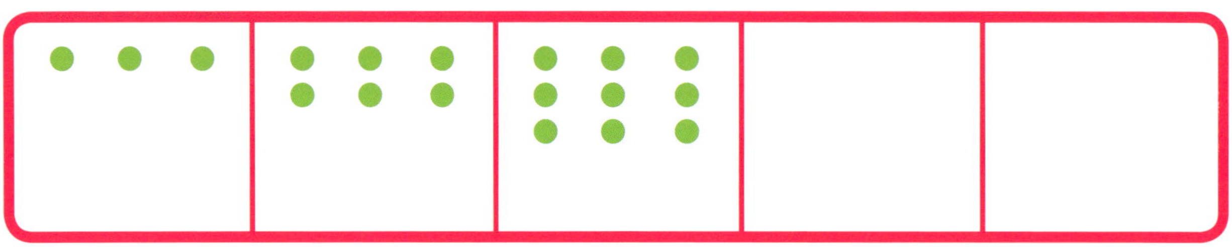

4 Complete this chart:

x	0	1	2	3	4	5	6	7	8	9	10
6				18							
9						45					

Extra challenge:

Can you work out the numbers in these sequences:

- start on 3 and multiply by 3 for 6 steps?
- start on 8 and double the number for 5 steps?

5 Fill in the missing numbers in each sequence:

80 72 ___ ___ ___ 40 ___ ___ ___ 8

60 56 52 ___ ___ ___ 36 ___ ___ ___

6 Continue this pattern:

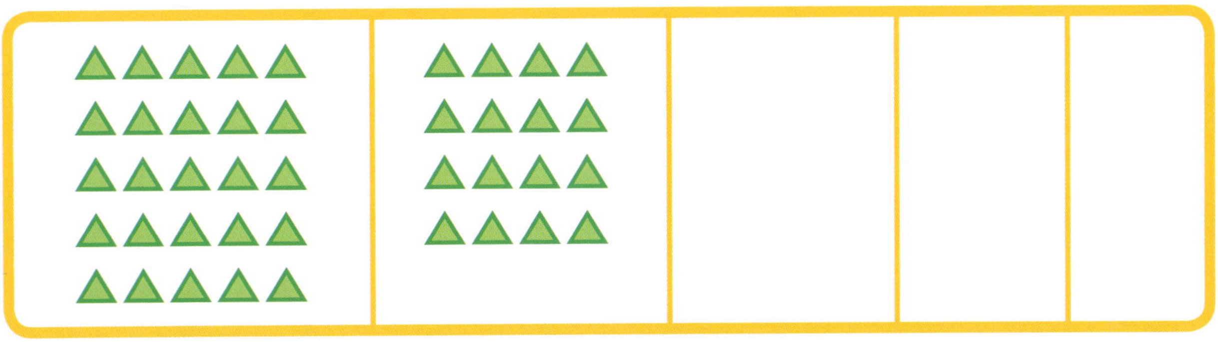

7 Complete this chart:

x	10	9	8	7	6	5	4	3	2	1	0
11			88								
12							48				

8 Complete each sequence:

200 190 180 ___ ___ ___ ___ ___ ___ ___

150 148 146 ___ ___ ___ ___ ___ ___ ___

Groups of 12

You know most of these.
They have been in the others,
So you can answer with ease.

1) A baker takes an hour to cook 12 loaves of bread. How many loaves can he make in 3 hours?

[ ] loaves

2) Complete each sequence:

0 12 24 [ ] [ ] [ ] [ ] [ ] [ ] [ ]

144 132 120 [ ] [ ] [ ] [ ] [ ] [ ] [ ]

60 72 84 [ ] [ ] [ ] [ ] [ ] [ ] [ ]

3) Answer these questions:

Five groups of twelve are [ ]

Eight times twelve is [ ]

Ten multiplied by twelve is [ ]

4) Cara collects trading cards. She buys 12 packs of 4 cards at £2 per pack. How much money does Cara spend and how many trading cards will she have?

[ ] [ ] trading cards

5) Work out these multiplication sums.

13	17	24	35	42	100
x 12	x 12	x 12	x 12	x 12	x 12
....	....	....	....	....	....

Extra challenge:
Another way to work out or check the answer to 12x a number is to multiply the number by 10, multiply the number by 2, and then add the two answers. For example: 14 x 12 = (14 x 10) + (14 x 2) = 140 + 28 = 168. Choose some 2-digit numbers and give this a go.

6 Divide each number by 12:

0 ☐ 48 ☐ 84 ☐ 132 ☐ 192 ☐

7 Mum has a loan of £864, which she pays back in equal amounts over 12 months. How much does Mum pay each month?

☐

8 How many shapes are there in each group?

☐ ☐

Dozen a day

Keep multiplying by 12 to find the way
To get the answers for a Dozen a day.

1. A dozen children split themselves equally into 3 teams to play a game. How many children are there in each team?

   [ ] children

2. Cupcakes were sold in boxes of 12. How many cupcakes were there in 15 boxes?

   [ ] cupcakes

3. How many dozen eggs are there in a gross of eggs? **Hint:** A gross is 144.

   [ ]

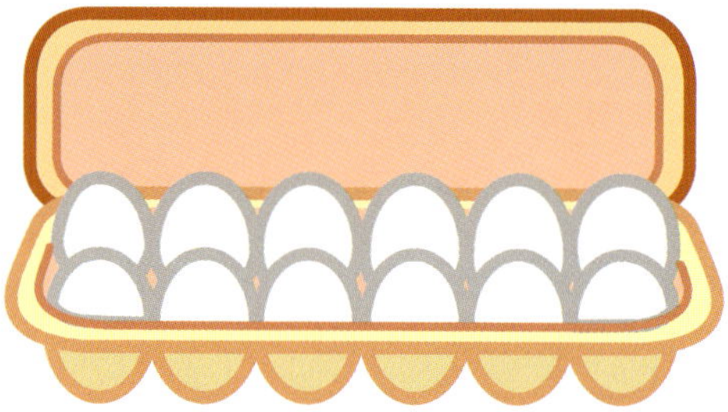

4. What are the factors of 12?

   [ ] [ ] [ ] [ ] [ ] [ ]

5. A score of children had 12 sweets each. How many sweets did they have altogether? **Note:** A score is 20.

   [ ] sweets

Extra challenge:
How many cartons of a dozen eggs will be needed to pack 216 eggs? 300 eggs? 432 eggs? How many eggs are there in 42 cartons, each with a dozen eggs?

6 A chef cooks a batch of 12 pancakes in 12 minutes. How many batches of 12 pancakes can he make in an hour?

[ ] batches

7 Trains arrived at Whistlestop Station 3 times an hour. How many trains arrived in 12 hours?

[ ] trains

8 A group of musicians performed a dozen pieces in a concert. Each piece lasted 4 minutes. How many minutes did the musicians perform altogether?

[ ]

9 900 raffle tickets were sold at a fund-raising event. There were a dozen prizes. What was the chance of winning a prize? Circle the correct answer.

1 in 50 1 in 75 1 in 100

10 Once a month, Jill ran a distance of 10 km in a cross-country event. How many kilometres did Jill run in a year?

[ ]

Plants

Flowers, fruits, vegetables and trees;
If you know your times tables,
You will answer these with ease.

1) A bee visits 47 flowers each trip before returning to its hive. How many flowers will it visit in 5 trips?

[ ] flowers

2) A tulip has 6 petals. How many petals will 24 tulips have altogether?

[ ] petals

3) A flower arranger used 112 poppies for her arrangement. Half were red, $\frac{3}{8}$ were yellow, and the rest were orange. How many poppies of each colour did the flower arranger use?

[ ] red [ ] yellow [ ] orange

4) A gardener plants 5 rows with 14 potatoes in each row. How many potato plants does that make altogether?

[ ] plants

5) Jim plants 2 bean seeds in each flower pot. He has 38 seeds in a packet. How many flower pots will Jim need?

[ ] pots

Extra challenge:
A gardener is planning his square garden. Calculate how many of each plant he needs: 4 rows of 8 fruit trees in each row; 7 shrubs for each side; 6 V-shaped rows of 12 flowers for each row; 5 plant pots with a tepee of 3 climbing plants in each.

6) A farmer grows 64 cabbages in each row.
How many cabbages does he grow in 12 rows?

[ ] cabbages

7) Nina's pumpkin weighs 22 kg, but Peter's pumpkin weighs 3 times as much. How much does Peter's pumpkin weigh?

[ ]

8) Vinny picks 340 apples. He puts an equal number into each of 4 crates.
How many apples are there in 1 crate?

[ ] apples

9) A tree seedling grows 60 cm a year. How tall will it be after 18 years?

[ ]

10) A pine tree is $\frac{1}{5}$ the height of a giant redwood tree, which is 115 m tall.

What is the height of the pine tree?

[ ]

Answer section

4

1. Anne has 2 baskets with 5 flowers in each basket.
How many flowers are there in total?
Fill in the numbers.

2 baskets × 5 flowers = 10 flowers

2. Complete each sequence:

2 4 6 8 10 12 14 16 18 20 22 24

48 46 44 42 40 38 36 34 32 30 28 26

54 56 58 60 62 64 66 68 70 72 74 76

3. Answer these questions:
Six multiplied by two is 12
Seven times two is 14
Nine groups of two are 18

4. A theatre ticket costs £24.50.
How much will 2 tickets cost?

£49.00

5. Work out these multiplication sums:

150	175	236	348	427	519
× 2	× 2	× 2	× 2	× 2	× 2
300	350	472	696	854	1 038

5

6. Divide each number by 2:

76 38   142 71   178 89

7. Work out these division sums:

$2\overline{)126}$ = 63 $2\overline{)240}$ = 120 $2\overline{)352}$ = 176 $2\overline{)684}$ = 342 $2\overline{)792}$ = 396

8. Fazir and Tira shared £7.80 equally between them.
How much money did each child receive?

£3.90

9. There were 284 bees in 2 hives. If there was an equal number in each hive, how many bees were there in 1 hive?

142 bees

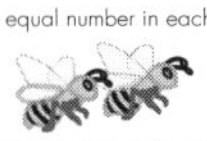

10. How many shapes are there in each group?

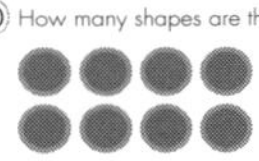

8

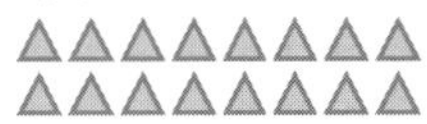

16

6

1. Double each number:

25 50   42 84   70 140   127 254

2. How many socks are there in 36 pairs?

72 socks

3. In a day, a factory makes wheels for 350 bicycles.
How many wheels are made in 1 day?

700 wheels

4. The table below shows some ingredients needed to make 12 biscuits.
Calculate how much of each you will need to make 24 biscuits.
Hint: Double each amount.

Ingredients	Quantity for 12 biscuits	Quantity for 24 biscuits
Flour	350g (12oz)	700g (24oz)
Eggs	2	4
Butter	225g (8oz)	450g (16oz)
Caster sugar	175g (6oz)	350g (12oz)
Dark chocolate	350g (12oz)	700g (24 oz)
Light brown sugar	175g (6oz)	350g (12oz)

7

5. How many wings do 275 crane flies have altogether?
Note: A crane fly has two wings.

550 wings

6. The chart shows the number of bunches of flowers sold in a store in one week.
Write the total for each day.

(flower) = 2 bunches

Day	Number of bunches sold	Total
Monday	10 × (flower)	20
Tuesday	8 × (flower)	16
Wednesday	12 × (flower)	24
Thursday	9 × (flower)	18
Friday	20 × (flower)	40
Saturday	14 × (flower)	28
Sunday	5 × (flower)	10

7. Ryan cycles 56km, but Jake cycles twice as far. How far does Jake cycle?

112km

8. Mum has spent £84.00 on presents for Jayden, but Dad has spent double that amount.
How much money has Dad spent?

£168.00

8

1. Tiya had 7 parcels. Each parcel weighed 10 kg. How much did the parcels weigh altogether?

70 kg

2. Complete these sequences:
10 20 30 **40 50 60 70 80 90 100**
150 140 130 **120 110 100 90 80 70 60**
270 280 290 **300 310 320 330 340 350 360**

3. Answer these questions:
Ten eights are **80**
Ten times ten is **100**
Nine multiplied by ten is **90**

4. Zina saved 35 10-pence coins. How much money did Zina have altogether?

£3.50

5. Work out these multiplication sums:

436	845	152	1 689	791	287
× 10	× 10	× 10	× 10	× 10	× 10
4 360	8 450	1 520	16 890	7 910	2 870

9

6. Divide each number by 10:
10 **1** 40 **4** 80 **8** 120 **12** 150 **15**

7. Work out these division sums:
$420 \div 10 =$ **42** $367 \div 10 =$ **36.7** $780 \div 10 =$ **78** $842 \div 10 =$ **84.2** $990 \div 10 =$ **99**

8. How many leaves are there in each group? **Hint:** Multiply the number of rows by the number of columns.

80 **70**

10

1. Multiply each number by 100:
4 **400** 47 **4 700** 470 **47 000** 4 070 **407 000**

2. A box contains 100 T-shirts. How many T-shirts are there in 64 boxes?

6 400 T-shirts

3. Multiply the number by 100 each time:
3 **300 30 000 3 000 000**
82 **8 200 820 000 82 000 000**

4. How many centimetres are there in 84 m? **8 400 cm**

5. Divide each number by 100:
42 000 **420** 702 000 **7 020**
804 200 **8 042** 6 000 000 **60 000**

11

6. Multiply each number by 1 000:
7 **7 000** 82 **82 000** 146 **146 000** 150 **150 000**

7. How many grams are there in 7.2 kg?
7 200 g

8. How many pence are there in £35?
3 500 p

9. A plane flies at a height of 10 668 m. What is this height in kilometres?

10.668 km

10. A colony of army ants has 700 000 ants. As the ants cross a river, 20% of the colony dies. How many ants make it across?
560 000 ants

12

1. A jar holds 8 biscuits. How many biscuits are there in 3 jars?
24 biscuits

2. Complete each sequence:
0 3 6 **9 12 15 18 21 24 27**
36 33 30 **27 24 21 18 15 12 9**
36 39 42 **45 48 51 54 57 60 63**

3. Answer these questions:
Three fives are **15**
Three multiplied by seven is **21**
Three times nine is **27**

4. Neo bought 6 oranges at 30 p each. What was the total cost of the 6 oranges?

£1.80

5. Work out these multiplication sums:

16	33	55	79	145	229
× 3	× 3	× 3	× 3	× 3	× 3
48	99	165	237	435	687

13

6. Divide each number by 3:
6 **2** 15 **5** 24 **8** 36 **12** 45 **15**

7. How long will it take Anita to save 42 p if she saves 3 p every week?
14 weeks

8. Work out these division sums:
$60 \div 3 =$ **20** $90 \div 3 =$ **30** $72 \div 3 =$ **24** $99 \div 3 =$ **33** $183 \div 3 =$ **61**

9. Pablo was paid £3 for each car that he washed. He earned £39 in one week. How many cars did Pablo wash that week?

13 cars

10. How many shapes are there in each group?

21 **27**

14

1. How many wheels are there on 15 tricycles?
45 wheels

2. How many sides do 55 triangles have?
165 sides

3. About 170 triplets are born in the United Kingdom each year. How many babies is this?
510 babies

4. Thirty-nine trimarans race in a competition. How many hulls are there altogether? **Note:** A trimaran is a boat with 3 hulls.
117 hulls

5. Fifty-four children are split into groups of 3. How many groups of children are there?
18 groups

6. A magnifying glass makes bugs look triple their size. Below are the original sizes of the bugs. What size is each of the bugs when it is magnified?
Worm: 6.5 cm **19.5 cm**

Centipede: 5.25 cm **15.75 cm**

Ladybird: 1.75 cm **5.25 cm**

15

7. Packets of biscuits are sold in boxes of 3 packets. This chart shows how many boxes are sold from a store in a week. Calculate the number of packets sold that week.
(1 box = 3 packets)

Day	Number of boxes	Total
Monday		6
Tuesday		15
Wednesday		12
Thursday		24
Friday		3
Saturday		27
Sunday		21

8. Leaving no spaces, fit 9 small triangles (of equal size) inside the large equilateral triangle.
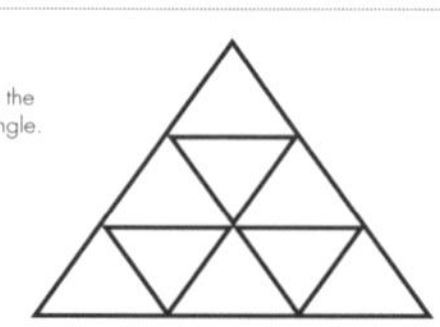

16

① Share 28 sweets equally among 4 children. How many sweets will each child get?

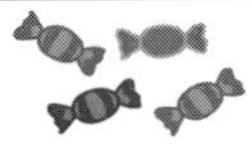

[7] sweets

② Complete each sequence:

0 4 8 [12] [16] [20] [24] [28] [32] [36]

48 44 40 [36] [32] [28] [24] [20] [16] [12]

52 56 60 [64] [68] [72] [76] [80] [84] [88]

③ Answer these questions:

Nine times four is [36]

Seven groups of four are [28]

Four fives are [20]

④ Dad took Devan, Jesse, and Owen to the fair. The roller coaster ride cost £1.50 for each person. How much did Dad have to pay for all of them to go on the ride?

[£6]

⑤ Work out these multiplication sums:

23	17	25	115	200	214
× 4	× 4	× 4	× 4	× 4	× 4
92	68	100	460	800	856

17

⑥ Divide each number by 4:

0 [0] 4 [1] 16 [4] 36 [9] 48 [12]

⑦ Jeff buys a pack of 4 pencils. The pack costs £1.68. How much does 1 pencil cost? [42p]

⑧ Work out these division sums:

4⟌56 [14] 4⟌96 [24] 4⟌100 [25] 4⟌128 [32] 4⟌284 [71]

⑨ A box contains 24 chocolates. They are laid out in 4 equal rows. How many chocolates are there in each row?

[6] chocolates

⑩ How many shapes are there in each group?

[12] [40]

18

① How many sides do these shapes have in total?

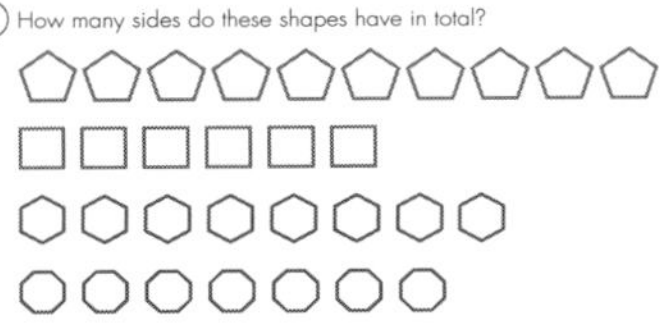

[50] [24] [48] [56]

② How many triangles have 27 angles in total?

[9] triangles

③ The inside angles of an equilateral triangle add up to 180°. What is the value of each angle?

[60°]

④ Each side of a regular hexagon is 7 cm. What is the perimeter of the hexagon?

[42 cm]

⑤ What is the area of a rectangle with a length of 11 cm and a breadth of 4 cm?

[44 cm²]

⑥ Each angle of a square is 90°. What is the total of the 4 angles?

[360°]

19

⑦ A cuboid has 8 vertices. How many cuboids will have a total of 80 vertices?

[10] cuboids

⑧ How many faces do these shapes have?

7 triangular prisms [35]

9 cuboids [54]

12 cylinders [36]

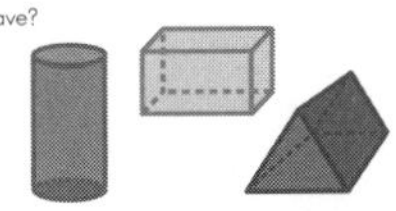

⑨ How many edges do these shapes have?

7 cubes [84]

4 square-based pyramids [32]

3 hexagonal prisms [54]

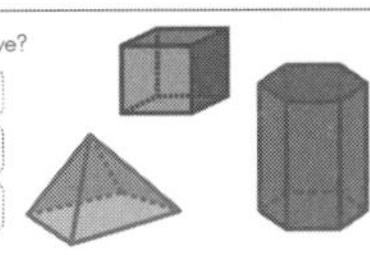

⑩ What is the volume of this cuboid?

Hint: Volume = length x breadth x height

[72 cm³]

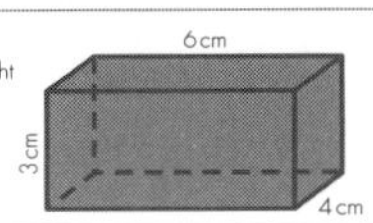

20

① A pack of greeting cards contains 5 cards. How many cards are there in 3 packs?

[15] cards

② Complete each sequence:

0 5 10 [15] [20] [25] [30] [35] [40] [45]

60 55 50 [45] [40] [35] [30] [25] [20] [15]

75 80 85 [90] [95] [100] [105] [110] [115] [120]

③ Answer these questions:

Five groups of six are [30]

Seven multiplied by five is [35]

Eleven times five is [55]

④ David saved 24 5-pence coins. How much money did David save?

[£1.20]

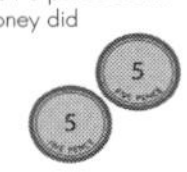

⑤ Work out these multiplication sums:

18	20	49	56	130	222
× 5	× 5	× 5	× 5	× 5	× 5
90	100	245	280	650	1 110

21

⑥ Divide each number by 5:

10 [2] 25 [5] 30 [6] 50 [10] 85 [17]

⑦ Five children are given £1.95 to share equally among them. How much money will each child receive? [39p]

⑧ Work out these division sums:

5⟌65 [13] 5⟌80 [16] 5⟌125 [25] 5⟌175 [35] 5⟌250 [50]

⑨ There are 270 children in a school. There are 5 years, and each year has an equal number of children. How many children are there in Year 4? [54] children

⑩ How many shapes are there in each group?

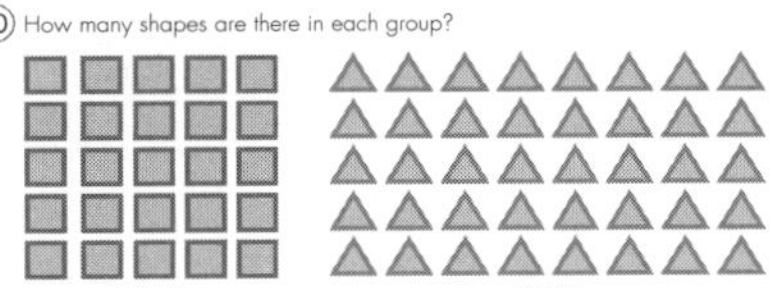

[25] [40]

22

① How many minutes are there in 4 hours?

[240 minutes]

② How many minutes is it past 11 o'clock?

[45 minutes]

③ How many minutes are there between 9.45 a.m. and 11.05 a.m.?

[80 minutes]

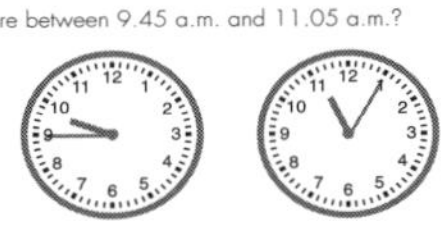

④ How many minutes are there in 1 day?

[1 440 minutes]

⑤ How many decades are there in half a century?

Note: A decade is 10 years; a century is 100 years.

[5] decades

23

⑥ How many hours are there in these months?

September (30 days) [720 hours] February (28 days) [672 hours]

May (31 days) [744 hours]

⑦ Write the number of minutes past the hour shown on each of these clocks.

[20 minutes] [55 minutes] [10 minutes] [35 minutes]

⑧ How many minutes are there between 3.10 p.m. and 5.25 p.m.?

[135 minutes]

24

1) 0 × 3 = 0 | 2) 12 × 2 = 24 | 3) 9 × 5 = 45
4) 1 × 4 = 4 | 5) 11 × 5 = 55 | 6) 3 × 4 = 12
7) 7 × 3 = 21 | 8) 10 × 2 = 20 | 9) 2 × 2 = 4
10) 6 × 5 = 30 | 11) 11 × 4 = 44 | 12) 8 × 2 = 16
13) 4 × 4 = 16 | 14) 10 × 5 = 50 | 15) 2 × 5 = 10
16) 6 × 3 = 18 | 17) 10 × 9 = 90 | 18) 9 × 4 = 36
19) 1 × 5 = 5 | 20) 12 × 4 = 48 | 21) 6 × 4 = 24
22) 7 × 4 = 28 | 23) 10 × 1 = 10 | 24) 12 × 10 = 120
25) 2 × 4 = 8 | 26) 10 × 7 = 70 | 27) 10 × 10 = 100
28) 8 × 4 = 32 | 29) 11 × 2 = 22 | 30) 0 × 2 = 0

25

31) 24 ÷ 3 = 8 | 32) 6 ÷ 2 = 3 | 33) 15 ÷ 5 = 3
34) 30 ÷ 5 = 6 | 35) 9 ÷ 3 = 3 | 36) 30 ÷ 10 = 3
37) 14 ÷ 2 = 7 | 38) 3 ÷ 3 = 1 | 39) 50 ÷ 10 = 5
40) 40 ÷ 5 = 8 | 41) 2 ÷ 2 = 1 | 42) 90 ÷ 10 = 9
43) 21 ÷ 3 = 7 | 44) 6 ÷ 3 = 2 | 45) 10 ÷ 10 = 1
46) 18 ÷ 2 = 9 | 47) 27 ÷ 3 = 9 | 48) 80 ÷ 10 = 8
49) 15 ÷ 5 = 3 | 50) 15 ÷ 3 = 5 | 51) 60 ÷ 10 = 6
52) 40 ÷ 8 = 5 | 53) 36 ÷ 3 = 12 | 54) 70 ÷ 10 = 7
55) 18 ÷ 3 = 6 | 56) 60 ÷ 5 = 12 | 57) 110 ÷ 10 = 11
58) 30 ÷ 3 = 10 | 59) 25 ÷ 5 = 5 | 60) 100 ÷ 10 = 10

26

1) A tube holds 6 tennis balls. How many balls will 8 tubes hold?

48 balls

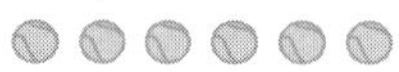

2) Complete each sequence:

0 6 12 18 24 30 36 42 48 54

72 66 60 54 48 42 36 30 24 18

54 60 66 72 78 84 90 96 102 108

3) Answer these questions:

Six threes are 18

Four multiplied by six is 24

Six groups of seven are 42

4) Selma bought 9 bananas at 6p each. How much money did she spend?

54p

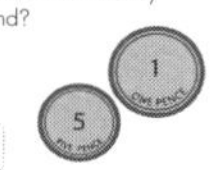

5) Work out these multiplication sums:

14	25	38	54	116	200
× 6	× 6	× 6	× 6	× 6	× 6
84	150	228	324	696	1 200

27

6) Divide each number by 6:

18 → 3 | 30 → 5 | 66 → 11 | 72 → 12 | 96 → 16

7) £2.50 is shared equally among 6 children. How much money is left over?

4p

8) 174 cars are parked in 6 rows of equal length. How many cars are there in each row?

29 cars

9) Work out these division sums:

6)90 = 15 | 6)102 = 17 | 6)204 = 34 | 6)276 = 46 | 6)348 = 58

10) How many items are there in each group?

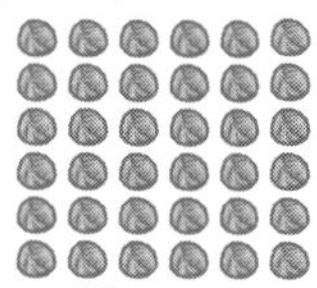

36 cabbages

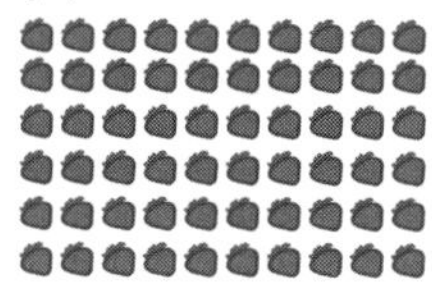

60 strawberries

28

1) Will recorded the number of bugs he saw in his garden in a month. How many legs did each type of insect have altogether?
Hint: An insect has 6 legs.

Name of bug	Number sighted	Total number of legs
Beetle	||||| ||||| ||||| ||	102
Wasp	||||| |||	48
Butterfly	||||| ||||| |||||	90
Ladybird	||||| ||||| ||||| |||||		126

2) If a desert locust eats 2 g of food each day, how much will a swarm of 66 million desert locusts eat in a day?

132 million g

3) A ladybird is about 6 mm long. Under the microscope, the ladybird is magnified 40 times. What size is the ladybird when seen through the microscope?

240 mm or 24 cm

4) A leaf-cutter ant travels 360 m each day. Altogether, what is the total distance the ant will travel in 60 days?

21 600 m or 21.6 km

29

5) How many wings does a swarm of 6 000 bees have altogether?
Hint: Bees have 4 wings.

24 000 wings

6) A queen wasp can lay 2 000 eggs a day. How many eggs can she lay in 60 days?

120 000 eggs

7) A butterfly lays 600 eggs, and only a quarter of them hatch into caterpillars. How many eggs **do not** hatch?

450 eggs

8) Class 5F went to a pond. They made a picture chart of the number of bugs they saw in the pond. How many bugs of each type did they see?

= 6 bugs = 3 bugs

Name of bug	Number of bugs	Total
Pond skaters		24
Water bugs		18
Whirligig beetles		15
Dragonfly nymphs		3
Water spiders		6

30

1) Adam ran 400 m in 59 seconds. Jonas took twice as long. How long did Jonas take?

118 seconds

2) Three cyclists raced at 58 mph, 63 mph, and 56 mph. What was their average speed?

59 mph

3) These were the results of a season's football games:
A win = 5 points, a draw = 3 points, and a loss = 1 point.
How many points did each team get?

Football team	Win	Loss	Draw	Points
England	8	2	5	57
United States	7	3	6	56
Japan	7	1	7	57
Brazil	9	2	4	59

4) The winner of a tennis tournament won 4 times the prize money of a semi-finalist. If a semi-finalist received £475 000, how much money did the winner receive?

£1 900 000

31

5) John threw a javelin a distance of 64 m. Amy threw the javelin an eighth ($\frac{1}{8}$) less than John's distance. How far did Amy throw?

56 m

6) Seven race car drivers have a total of 1 645 points. What is the average number of points scored?

235 points

7) There were 162 rounders players taking part in a tournament. Each team had 9 players. How many teams were there?

18 teams

8) The length of a swimming pool is 25 m. This chart shows how many times each child swam that length. How far did each child swim?

Name of child	Number of lengths	Total distance
Harry	10	250 m
Jasmine	8	200 m
Jamie	6	150 m
Heidi	5	125 m

32

1. A dog eats 3 dog treats a day. How many treats will it eat in 7 days?

21 treats

2. Complete each sequence:

0, 7, 14, 21, 28, 35, 42, 49, 56, 63

84, 77, 70, 63, 56, 49, 42, 35, 28, 21

35, 42, 49, 56, 63, 70, 77, 84, 91, 98

3. Answer these questions:

Seven sixes are 42

Eight multiplied by seven is 56

Five groups of seven are 35

4. A train ticket costs £7. How much will 6 tickets cost?

£42

5. Work out these multiplication sums:

14	20	35	59	123	246
× 7	× 7	× 7	× 7	× 7	× 7
98	140	245	413	861	1 722

33

6. Divide each number by 7:

0 → 0, 21 → 3, 49 → 7, 77 → 11, 98 → 14

7. Seven books cost £35.84 altogether. If each book was the same price, what was the price of 1 book?

£5.12

8. Work out these division sums:

$84 \div 7 = 12$, $140 \div 7 = 20$, $105 \div 7 = 15$, $133 \div 7 = 19$, $224 \div 7 = 32$

9. Share 42 chairs equally around 7 tables. How many chairs will you keep around each table?

6 chairs

10. How many shapes are there in each group?

49

21

34

1. How many days are there in 15 weeks?

105 days

2. How many weeks are there in 7 years?

364 weeks

3. How many hours are there in a week?

168 hours

4. Dad works 35 hours a week. How many hours does he work over 4 weeks?

140 hours

5. Fran cycles for 30 minutes every day. How many minutes does she cycle in one week?

210 minutes

6. A bookshop opens for 7 hours each day from Monday to Saturday. How many hours is it open in one week?

42 hours

35

7. Chris practises on the keyboard for 105 minutes every week. He does an equal amount of time every day. How long is each practice?

15 minutes

8. Ella travelled for 91 days. How many weeks is this?

13 weeks

9. Dad books a holiday 22 weeks before going. How many days does the family have to wait?

154 days

10. How long in minutes does Kim do these daily activities in one week?

Watching 45 minutes of television: 315 minutes

Playing 30 minutes of computer games: 210 minutes

Reading for 1 hour 10 minutes: 490 minutes

36

1. Multiply the two numbers shown on the dice:

⚃ × ⚅ = 24   ⚄ × ⚄ = 25

⚂ × ⚃ = 12   ⚁ × ⚂ = 6

2. Add the numbers shown on the dice, and then multiply your answer by 6.

{⚀ + ⚃} × 6 = 30   {⚁ + ⚄} × 6 = 42

{⚅ + ⚅} × 6 = 72   {⚄ + ⚂} × 6 = 48

3. Jack threw a double six 5 times. What was his total?

60

4. These are the scores of four players. They each need to throw a double to reach 100 points. What is the number that needs to appear on both dice for each player? Fill in the spaces in the table.

Player	Score	Number required on both dice
1	90	5
2	98	1
3	94	3
4	88	6

37

5. Jess throws a die 100 times and records her scores. What is the total amount scored altogether by Jess? Fill in the spaces in the table.

Number on die	Number of times thrown	Total
1	卌 卌 卌 |	16
2	卌 卌 卌 卌	40
3	卌 卌 卌 |||	54
4	卌 卌 卌	60
5	卌 卌 卌 ||	85
6	卌 卌 ||||	84
	Total	339

6. A full deck of cards has 13 cards of each suit.

Note: There are 4 suits in a deck.

How many cards are there in a deck? 52 cards

How many cards are there in

4 decks? 208 cards

9 decks? 468 cards

6 decks? 312 cards

Multiply each of these cards by 8:

9 hearts: 72

8 diamonds: 64

Queen (12) clubs: 96

38

1. Six trains run every hour. Each train pulls 8 carriages. How many carriages are pulled every hour?

48 carriages

2. Complete these sequences:

0, 8, 16, 24, 32, 40, 48, 56, 64, 72

96, 88, 80, 72, 64, 56, 48, 40, 32, 24

40, 48, 56, 64, 72, 80, 88, 96, 104, 112

3. Answer these questions:

Eight sixes are 48

Two multiplied by eight is 16

Nine times eight is 72

4. A bag of apples costs £1.46. How much will 8 bags cost?

£11.68

5. Work out these multiplication sums:

15	24	48	97	120	236
× 8	× 8	× 8	× 8	× 8	× 8
120	192	384	776	960	1 888

39

6. Work out these division sums:

$96 \div 8 = 12$, $144 \div 8 = 18$, $168 \div 8 = 21$, $256 \div 8 = 32$, $312 \div 8 = 39$

7. Tammy needs 192 m of fencing to go around her garden. Each fencing panel is 8 m long. How many panels will she need?

24 panels

8. Perry pays £2.80 for 8 pencils. How much did 1 pencil cost?

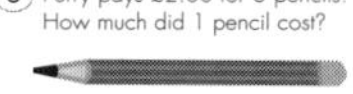

35p

9. Divide each number by 8:

0 → 0, 24 → 3, 56 → 7, 80 → 10, 96 → 12

10. How many gems are there in each group?

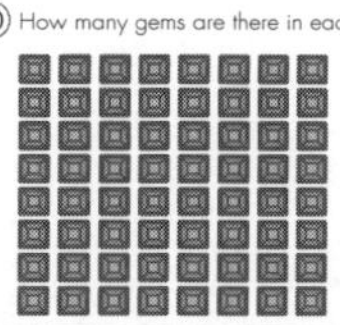

64

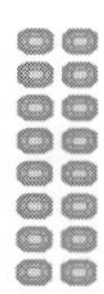

16

40

1. Thirty-five satellites are launched into orbit each year. How many satellites have been launched in 8 years?

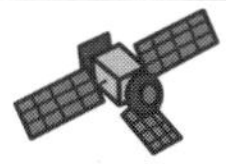

280 satellites

2. A probe travelling at 500 mph will take 8 years to get to Mars. How fast does the probe need to travel to get there in 1 year?

4 000 mph

3. Mars takes approximately 687 days to orbit the Sun. How many days will it take for Mars to orbit the Sun 8 times?

5 496 days

4. Neptune takes 165 years to orbit the Sun. How many years will it take to go around the Sun 8 times?

1 320 years

5. Mercury takes 88 Earth days to orbit the Sun. How many times will Mercury go around the Sun in 880 Earth days?

10 times

41

6. Multiply the 8 moons of Neptune with the 16 moons of Jupiter.

128 moons

7. The midday surface temperature of Mercury is 420°C. What is 8 times hotter than the surface of Mercury?

3 360°C

8. Mercury is 4 878km in diameter. What is an eighth ($\frac{1}{8}$) of its diameter?

609.75km

9. One day on Saturn lasts 10 hours and 14 minutes on Earth. How long in Earth time will 8 days on Saturn last?

81 hours 52 minutes

One day on Uranus lasts 17 hours and 8 minutes on Earth. How long in Earth time will 8 days on Saturn last?

137 hours 4 minutes

10. Saturn is 1.4 billion km away from the Sun. What is $\frac{5}{8}$ of this distance?

875 million km

Jupiter is 780 million km away from the Sun. What is $\frac{3}{8}$ of this distance?

292.5 million km

42

1. What is half ($\frac{1}{2}$) of each number?

18 → 9 10 → 5 6 → 3 24 → 12

2. What is a third ($\frac{1}{3}$) of each amount?

12g → 4g 27g → 9g 33g → 11g 42g → 14g

3. What is a quarter ($\frac{1}{4}$) of each number?

4 → 1 20 → 5 36 → 9 52 → 13

4. There are 60 carrots in a box. How many carrots make up...

$\frac{7}{10}$ of the box? 42 carrots

$\frac{1}{10}$ of the box? 6 carrots

$\frac{2}{10}$ of the box? 12 carrots

5. There were 25 bananas, and $\frac{1}{5}$ were eaten. How many bananas are left?

20 bananas

43

6. What is three quarters ($\frac{3}{4}$) of each number?

12 → 9 24 → 18 32 → 24 44 → 33

7. What is $\frac{1}{8}$ of 48 slices of pizza?

6 slices

8. What is $\frac{7}{10}$ of 40?

28

9. There are 30 children in a class. $\frac{3}{5}$ of the class have school dinners. How many children **do not** have school dinners?

12 children

10. Oliver picked 54 apples. $\frac{1}{6}$ were rotten. How many apples were rotten?

9 apples

44

1. There are 8 horse races in a day. If 9 different horses took part in each race, how many horses ran that day?

72 horses

2. Complete each sequence:

0 9 18 27 36 45 54 63 72 81

108 99 90 81 72 63 54 45 36 27

45 54 63 72 81 90 99 108 117 126

3. Answer these questions:

Three multiplied by nine is 27

Nine eights are 72

Six groups of nine are 54

4. A bunch of flowers costs £4.99. How much will 9 bunches cost?

£44.91

5. Work out these multiplication sums:

16 × 9 = 144

23 × 9 = 207

92 × 9 = 828

47 × 9 = 423

150 × 9 = 1 350

218 × 9 = 1 962

45

6. Divide each number by 9:

9 → 1 36 → 4 45 → 5 90 → 10 108 → 12

7. Jake needed £468 to buy a new television. He decided to save an equal amount over 9 weeks to reach the total. What is the amount he needed to save each week?

£52

8. How many shapes are there in each group?

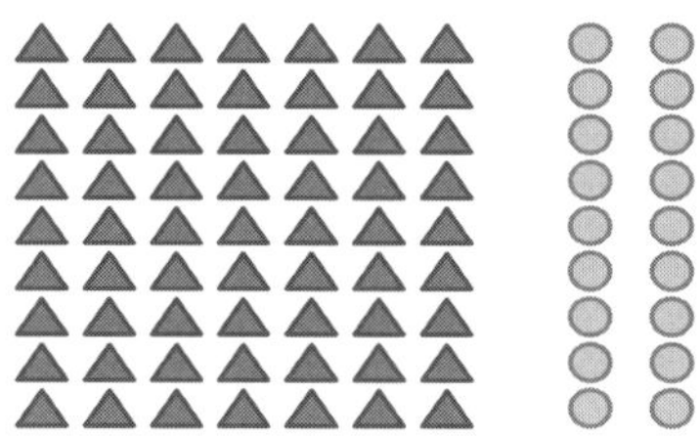

63 18

46

1. Calculate the total cost that Karl spent shopping.

Item	Cost per item	Amount	Total
Tomatoes	20p	6	£1.20
Carrots	10p	8	£0.80
Cabbage	89p	2	£1.78
Peppers	43p	5	£2.15
Cheese	£1.26	1	£1.26
Bread	76p	3	£2.28
Juice	£1.49	4	£5.96
Milk	72p	6	£4.32
Biscuits	89p	7	£6.23
Pasta	£2.56	2	£5.12
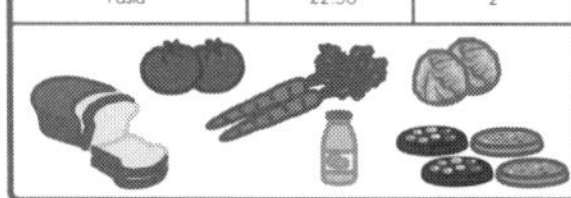			£31.10

47

2. A shopkeeper sold 6 red coats at £89 each. How much did the red coats cost altogether?

£534

3. Mum bought 3 bracelets at £7.84 each. How much money did Mum spend?

£23.52

4. Tami spent £77.97 on 3 pairs of shoes. Each pair cost the same amount. How much did each pair cost?

£25.99

5. In a sale, the cost of a hat was reduced by 20%. The original price of the hat was £14.50. How much was it reduced by?

£2.90

48

(1) Match each question to its answer:

168 ÷ 6 → 28
524 ÷ 4 → 131
595 ÷ 7 → 85
729 ÷ 9 → 81

(2) Use the long division method to work out each sum:

$4\overline{)648} = 162$ (−4, 24, −24, 08, −08, 0)

$2\overline{)496} = 248$ (−4, 09, −08, 16, −16, 0)

$5\overline{)760} = 152$ (−5, 26, −25, 10, −10, 0)

$6\overline{)822} = 137$ (−6, 22, −18, 42, −42, 0)

(3) What is the remainder each time?

592 ÷ 3 [1]
264 ÷ 7 [5]
786 ÷ 4 [2]
543 ÷ 9 [3]

(4) Circle all the multiples of 7:

(14) 23 (35) 43 76 (84)

49

(5) Circle all the multiples of 9:

28 (54) 61 83 (99) (108)

(6) Circle all the multiples of 12:

(24) 45 (60) 56 (72) 98 (132)

(7) Work out these money sums:

£14.58 ÷ 3 = [£4.86]
£35.60 ÷ 8 = [£4.45]
£26.96 ÷ 4 = [£6.74]
£66.69 ÷ 9 = [£7.41]

(8) List all the factors for each number:

24: 1, 2, 3, 4, 6, 8, 12, 24
36: 1, 2, 3, 4, 6, 9, 12, 18, 36
72: 1, 2, 3, 4, 6, 8, 9, 12, 18, 24, 36, 72
100: 1, 2, 4, 5, 10, 20, 25, 50, 100

50

(1) 0 × 9 = 0	(2) 0 × 6 = 0	(3) 8 × 9 = 72
(4) 5 × 8 = 40	(5) 7 × 8 = 56	(6) 3 × 8 = 24
(7) 2 × 9 = 18	(8) 7 × 6 = 42	(9) 2 × 7 = 14
(10) 1 × 7 = 7	(11) 9 × 9 = 81	(12) 10 × 9 = 90
(13) 2 × 8 = 16	(14) 1 × 8 = 8	(15) 12 × 6 = 72
(16) 3 × 6 = 18	(17) 9 × 7 = 63	(18) 10 × 7 = 70
(19) 4 × 7 = 28	(20) 4 × 9 = 36	(21) 11 × 6 = 66
(22) 8 × 8 = 64	(23) 6 × 8 = 48	(24) 11 × 8 = 88
(25) 9 × 6 = 54	(26) 6 × 7 = 42	(27) 12 × 7 = 84
(28) 5 × 6 = 30	(29) 7 × 7 = 49	(30) 12 × 9 = 108

51

(31) 0 ÷ 7 = 0	(32) 60 ÷ 6 = 10	(33) 63 ÷ 9 = 7
(34) 0 ÷ 8 = 0	(35) 99 ÷ 9 = 11	(36) 84 ÷ 7 = 12
(37) 9 ÷ 9 = 1	(38) 27 ÷ 9 = 3	(39) 48 ÷ 8 = 6
(40) 6 ÷ 6 = 1	(41) 96 ÷ 8 = 12	(42) 72 ÷ 8 = 9
(43) 21 ÷ 7 = 3	(44) 32 ÷ 8 = 4	(45) 63 ÷ 7 = 9
(46) 24 ÷ 6 = 4	(47) 45 ÷ 9 = 5	(48) 35 ÷ 7 = 5
(49) 77 ÷ 7 = 11	(50) 48 ÷ 6 = 8	(51) 54 ÷ 9 = 6
(52) 80 ÷ 8 = 10	(53) 49 ÷ 7 = 7	(54) 12 ÷ 6 = 2
(55) 36 ÷ 6 = 6	(56) 64 ÷ 8 = 8	(57) 56 ÷ 7 = 8
(58) 40 ÷ 8 = 5	(59) 81 ÷ 9 = 9	(60) 108 ÷ 9 = 12

52

(1) A farmer plants 6 rows of tulips, with 11 bulbs in each row. How many tulip bulbs are planted?

[66] bulbs

(2) Complete each sequence:

0, 11, 22, [33], [44], [55], [66], [77], [88], [99]
143, 132, 121, [110], [99], [88], [77], [66], [55], [44]
66, 77, 88, [99], [110], [121], [132], [143], [154], [165]

(3) Answer these questions:

Eleven fours are [44]
Eleven groups of seven are [77]
Twelve times eleven is [132]

(4) Ellie buys 11 T-shirts at £1.10 each. How much does Ellie pay for 11 T-shirts?

[£12.10]

(5) Work out these multiplication sums:

14	25	69	33	81	100
× 11	× 11	× 11	× 11	× 11	× 11
154	275	759	363	891	1 100

53

(6) Divide each number by 11:

22 [2] 88 [8] 121 [11] 143 [13] 176 [16]

(7) Work out these division sums:

$11\overline{)187} = 17$ $11\overline{)297} = 27$ $11\overline{)363} = 33$ $11\overline{)572} = 52$ $11\overline{)781} = 71$

(8) How many spots are there in each group?

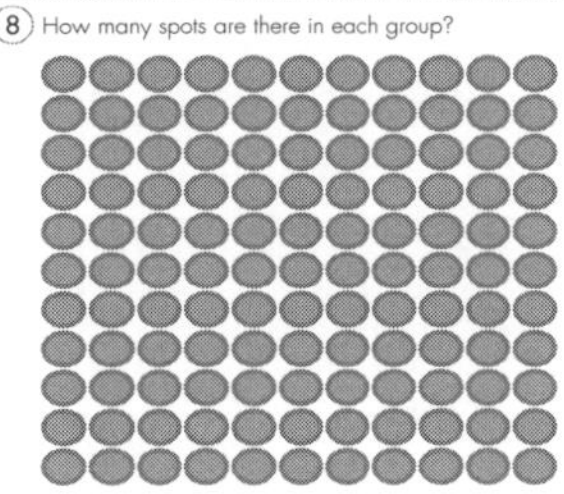

[121]

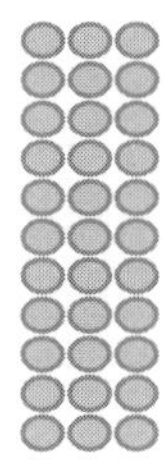

[33]

54

(1) Each stairway of an apartment building has 12 steps. How many steps are there in 6 stairways?

[72] steps

(2) A window cleaner takes 1 hour to clean 20 windows. How long will it take him to clean 120 windows?

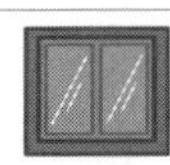

[6 hours]

(3) There are 210 windows in a 7-storey office building. There is an equal number of windows on each storey. How many windows are there on the fifth storey?

[30] windows

(4) An apartment building has 15 storeys and 6 flats on each storey. How many flats are there altogether?

[90] flats

(5) A school has 4 blocks with 9 classrooms in each block. How many classrooms are there altogether?

[36] classrooms

55

(6) A builder uses 500 tiles to cover half a roof of a house. How many tiles will he need for 6 houses?

[6 000] tiles

(7) A 10-storey hotel has a total of 378 rooms. The rooms are on floors 2 to 10. If there is an equal number of rooms on each floor, how many rooms are there on the eighth floor?

[42] rooms

(8) A house costs £285 000. The estate agent receives 5% of the sale price. How much money does the agent receive?

[£14 250]

(9) Two-thirds ($\frac{2}{3}$) of the 126 houses on Grove Avenue have garages. How many houses **do not** have garages?

[42] houses

(10) A shop has an area of $620\,m^2$. If the width of the shop is 20 m, what is its length?

[31 m]

56

(1) Fill in the missing numbers in each sequence:

5 10 [15] [20] [25] 30 [35] [40] 45 [50]

60 [65] [70] 75 [80] [85] [90] 95 [100] 105

(2) Complete each sequence:

4 8 12 [16] [20] [24] [28] [32] [36] [40]

7 14 21 [28] [35] [42] [49] [56] [63] [70]

25 50 75 [100] [125] [150] [175] [200] [225] [250]

(3) Continue this pattern:

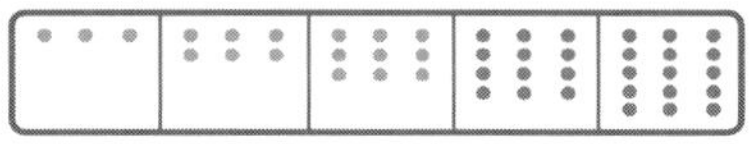

(4) Complete this chart:

x	0	1	2	3	4	5	6	7	8	9	10
6	0	6	12	18	24	30	36	42	48	54	60
9	0	9	18	27	36	45	54	63	72	81	90

57

(5) Fill in the missing numbers in each sequence:

80 72 [64] [56] [48] 40 [32] [24] [16] 8

60 56 52 [48] [44] [40] 36 [32] [28] [24]

(6) Continue this pattern:

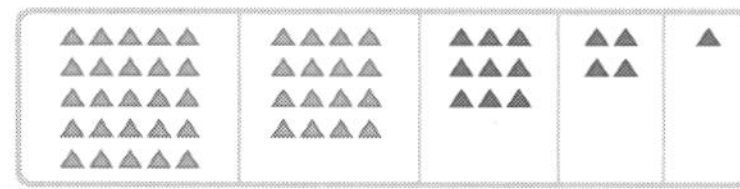

(7) Complete this chart:

x	10	9	8	7	6	5	4	3	2	1	0
11	110	99	88	77	66	55	44	33	22	11	0
12	120	108	96	84	72	60	48	36	24	12	0

(8) Complete each sequence:

200 190 180 [170] [160] [150] [140] [130] [120] [110]

150 148 146 [144] [142] [140] [138] [136] [134] [132]

58

(1) A baker takes an hour to cook 12 loaves of bread. How many loaves can he make in 3 hours?

[36] loaves

(2) Complete each sequence:

0 12 24 [36] [48] [60] [72] [84] [96] [108]

144 132 120 [108] [96] [84] [72] [60] [48] [36]

60 72 84 [96] [108] [120] [132] [144] [156] [168]

(3) Answer these questions:

Five groups of twelve are [60]

Eight times twelve is [96]

Ten multiplied by twelve is [120]

(4) Cara collects trading cards. She buys 12 packs of 4 cards at £2 per pack. How much money does Cara spend and how many trading cards will she have?

[£24] [48] trading cards

(5) Work out these multiplication sums.

13	17	24	35	42	100
x 12	x 12	x 12	x 12	x 12	x 12
156	204	288	420	504	1 200

59

(6) Divide each number by 12:

0 [0] 48 [4] 84 [7] 132 [11] 192 [16]

(7) Mum has a loan of £864, which she pays back in equal amounts over 12 months. How much does Mum pay each month?

[£72.00]

(8) How many shapes are there in each group?

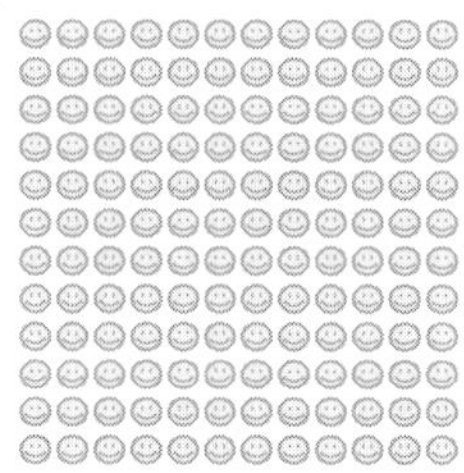

[144] [60]

60

(1) A dozen children split themselves equally into 3 teams to play a game. How many children are there in each team?

[4] children

(2) Cupcakes were sold in boxes of 12. How many cupcakes were there in 15 boxes?

[180] cupcakes

(3) How many dozen eggs are there in a gross of eggs? **Hint:** A gross is 144.

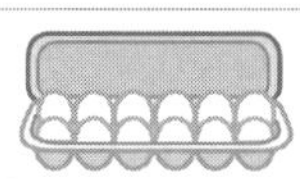

[12 dozen]

(4) What are the factors of 12?

[1] [2] [3] [4] [6] [12]

(5) A score of children had 12 sweets each. How many sweets did they have altogether? **Note:** A score is 20.

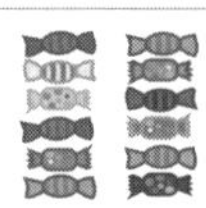

[240] sweets

61

(6) A chef cooks a batch of 12 pancakes in 12 minutes. How many batches of 12 pancakes can he make in an hour?

[5] batches

(7) Trains arrived at Whistlestop Station 3 times an hour. How many trains arrived in 12 hours?

[36] trains

(8) A group of musicians performed a dozen pieces in a concert. Each piece lasted 4 minutes. How many minutes did the musicians perform altogether?

[48 minutes]

(9) 900 raffle tickets were sold at a fund-raising event. There were a dozen prizes. What was the chance of winning a prize? Circle the correct answer.

1 in 50 (1 in 75) 1 in 100

(10) Once a month, Jill ran a distance of 10 km in a cross-country event. How many kilometres did Jill run in a year?

[120 km]

62

(1) A bee visits 47 flowers each trip before returning to its hive. How many flowers will it visit in 5 trips?

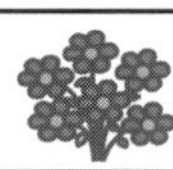

[235] flowers

(2) A tulip has 6 petals. How many petals will 24 tulips have altogether?

[144] petals

(3) A flower arranger used 112 poppies for her arrangement. Half were red, $\frac{3}{8}$ were yellow, and the rest were orange. How many poppies of each colour did the flower arranger use?

[56] red [42] yellow [14] orange

(4) A gardener plants 5 rows with 14 potatoes in each row. How many potato plants does that make altogether?

[70] plants

(5) Jim plants 2 bean seeds in each flower pot. He has 38 seeds in a packet. How many flower pots will Jim need?

[19] pots

63

(6) A farmer grows 64 cabbages in each row. How many cabbages does he grow in 12 rows?

[768] cabbages

(7) Nina's pumpkin weighs 22 kg, but Peter's pumpkin weighs 3 times as much. How much does Peter's pumpkin weigh?

[66 kg]

(8) Vinny picks 340 apples. He puts an equal number into each of 4 crates. How many apples are there in 1 crate?

[85] apples

(9) A tree seedling grows 60 cm a year. How tall will it be after 18 years?

[1 080 cm or 10.8 m]

(10) A pine tree is $\frac{1}{5}$ the height of a giant redwood tree, which is 115 m tall. What is the height of the pine tree?

[23 m]